P R A I S
M O T H E R H O O D

"Thank goodness! At last, a book that encourages mothers to strive for imperfection. We can succeed at that!"
—Dawn French, Comedienne, British TV star/writer *"The Vicar of Dibley," "French and Saunders,"* • *"Absolutely Fabulous,"* starring in *"Harry Potter III"*

"Beyond the dictates of dogma, beyond the despair of self-doubt, Motherhood Confidential takes us to a place where insight and authenticity are the true authorities."
—Ayelet Waldman, author, *Daughter's Keeper* and the *"Mommy-track Mystery Series"*

"You don't have to be a mother to love (and need) this book. It's a funny, moving, literate story of surviving the pressures of modern life, and still managing to preserve individuality, honesty, artistry and faith in one's intuition. And it's an intimate, inspiring portrait of that other treasured female experience –a best friendship."
—Judith Weston, author, *Directing Actors* and *The Film Director's Intuition*

"This unflinching co-memoir… goes where few books have dared, revealing what happens when intelligent women crash headlong into the often dogmatic expectations of American motherhood."
—Joni Golden, Michigan Women's Forum

"Delightful! Many mothers will commiserate with the authors' bare-all mothering journey."
—Sharon Heller, Ph.D., author, *Too Loud, Too Bright, Too Fast, Too Tight,* and *The Vital Touch: How Intimate Contact with Your Baby Leads to Healthier, Happier Development*

"Where's the sequel? I have to know what happens next! I want all my friends to read this book, whether they're mothers or not. Even though these women are nutty, they're able to come through for each other. From the first paragraph I was hooked."
—Elizabeth Kaye, singer, actress, teacher

"Thank heavens for women who are introspective, self-forgiving, and who know how to reach out to other women with a leg up from guilt and the too high standards we set for ourselves."
—Valerie Kack, Ph.D., LCSW, author
The Emotions Handbook

"Hilarious and unnervingly honest, a real page-turner."
—Cynthia Medeiros, artist, founder, Hummingbird Studio for Young Artists. Los Angeles

"This was the best book I've read in so long. And I read a lot. The way you combined comedy with gut-wrenching honesty was so refreshing. Finally something written about homeschooling that doesn't involve a whip and a desk or the other extreme—unschooling without parenting. I will be ordering more copies for my friends."

—Shawna Cryer, homeschooling mother, draftsman, photographer

"Gives a clear picture of the roller coaster of emotions all moms go through and maybe all friendships. It inspired me to reconnect with friendships which got lost in motherhood. I could see this as a musical, Martin Charnin and Charles Strouse could write the songs. "

—Barbara McDonald, mother of two, graveyard shift designer and illustrator

"This highly entertaining book puts a real face on today's mom. It encouraged me to be more "myself." I couldn't put the book down once it arrived in the mail."

—Judy Barrantes, homeschooling mother of two, Livermore, CA

MOTHERHOOD CONFIDENTIAL

The Strange Disappearance of My Best Friend

by Linda Cohen and Joan Bechtel

Thank you, Amy!

With love,
Joan Bechtel

© 2005 Linda Cohen and Joan Bechtel
Published by SocioPathways, an imprint of GynaVision
www.MotherhoodConfidential.com
ISBN.0-9760930-0-6
Printed in the United States of America August 2005

Publisher's Cataloging-in-Publication
(Provided by Quality Books, Inc.)

Cohen, Linda,
Motherhood confidential : the strange disappearance of my best friend / by
Linda Cohen and Joan Bechtel.
              p. cm.
       LCCN 2005921073
          ISBN 0-9760930-0-6
    1. Motherhood. 2. Cohen, Linda, 3. Bechtel, Joan. 4. Mothers—United
States—Biography. I. Bechtel, Joan. II. Title.

      HQ759.C65 2005   306.874'3
                                QBI05-200045

The following trademarks appear in this book: Coca Cola, Coke, Prozac,
Jack-in-the-Box, Chucky Cheese, Sony.

*We dedicate this book to our children
and to every mother trying to find her own way.*

We wish to thank the friends and family who supported us in the writing of this book:

Peggy Bechtel, Graham Barth, Tim Bechtel, Patricia Mittone, Jack Buckley, Brian Buckley, Colleen Sell, Thomas Barth, Michelle Grajkowski, Elizabeth Kaye, Robb Williams, Mary Kotsenas Williams, Anita Merzel, Belinda Vidaurri, Suzanne Mantell, Anita Frankel, Judith Weston, Cynthia Medeiros, Sonia Sickand, Stewart Latham, Jennifer Repo, Neil Cardew-Fanning

Contents

Sometimes our light goes out
but is blown back into flame
by another human being.
Each of us owes deepest thanks
to those who rekindled that light.
—*Albert Schweitzer*

One of the blessings of true friends
is that you can afford to be stupid with them.
—*Ralph Waldo Emerson*

I noticed your hostility toward him.
I ought to have guessed you were friends.
—*Malcom Bradbury*

PREFACE:
ONE SIZE FITS ALL?

(or Look Back in Anguish)

in which Linda opens Pandora's mother's box...

FASCINATING MOTHERHOOD PRE-TEST

PLEASE ANSWER THE FOLLOWING:

1. How could I be so self-centered to even consider
_____!

2. Why would anybody (except me) let their child
_____?

3. What kind of a mother am I anyway?
a. irresponsible
b. over-controlling
c. insane

Now for Part 2.

FASCINATING GIRLFRIEND PRE-TEST

1. Now that she has a child, she's so
(circle one) **sensitive, distant, judgmental.**

**2. Why does she have to prove how superior she is
by _____?**

**3. What kind of a mother is she anyway?
a. irresponsible
b. over-controlling
c. insane**

Times up. Pencils down.

Don't worry about grading. The answers don't matter. It's the anxiety that counts.

Eight years ago, I had no idea how many petals of angst motherhood could unfold. I was simply thrilled about the idea of having a child and joining that special community of women, of which my best friend, Joan, was already a two-generation card-carrying member. I was certain that Joan and I would become even closer than we were, which was pretty darn close.

Yet when our babies, Jack and Graham, came along, we found ourselves polar opposites on the spectrum of mothering. Joan wanted to mother her very needy child more than she felt society would approve of, and I longed for more freedom than seemed "acceptable." I couldn't fully comprehend her difficulties, and she seemed unable to understand mine.

Joan was dealing with the lonely life of an overwhelmed stay-at-home single mom in a remote mountain community. I was facing my own conflicts as a married working mother and unpublished writer in Los Angeles, bombarded by incessant reminders of everybody else's Hollywood success. But underneath all that we were so alike! How could motherhood be pulling us apart? Wasn't it supposed to unite us in a tribal bond of sisterhood?

Becoming a mother may be idealized as a fulfilling journey guided by ancestral instincts, modern science and a supportive community. But in Motherland nothing is as it "should be." The science of child-rearing can be overbearing, the community unsympathetic, and instincts virtually nonexistent. A whole village of alienation. The sisterhood of motherhood can feel more like a nasty seventh grade clique than a comforting Old Girls' Network.

If living up to a standard of perfection is the goal, it just might be that the true measure of a mother is her capacity for guilt and repression. Guilt to keep her from doing what's "not right," and repression to keep all those "not right" feelings in the closet.

But it's like trying to wear the Perfection Suit. It looks good and gets a lot of outside approval, but you can't breathe. You can't even squeeze into it unless you do some radical psychological liposuction. If you're handy with the power tools of sublimation surgery you can shed those ugly pounds of selfhood, wisdom, and authenticity you've put on over the years. For awhile anyway.

Maybe there are some mothers who can repress their way to sainthood. But those of us less well-endowed in that area (probably a lot of us) always seem to wind up straddling the dark chasm of self-doubt between what's *supposed to be* right and what deep down secretly *feels* right. The blowhole of maternal conflict.

The problem for me has been that we're more than just caretakers of our children—we're also women with different personalities, distinct histories and inner lives, each in the process of her own unique evolution. Who among us is "normal?" And, oh—all those dark emotions we're not supposed to have! And if we have them, we certainly shouldn't complain. Right? Just ship them off to the seedy back-alleys of Motherhood Noir.

My trials in that forbidden territory began as soon as I became pregnant. Was I supposed to pretend my inner conflicts didn't exist, or accept them as evidence that I was immature or unfit? What I needed was the kind of reassurance and empathy only a close girlfriend could give!

Joan and I first met when we were cast as best friends in a theatre production in Santa Cruz, California. During "Make It Like the Movies," life imitated art and we became best friends in real life, working together on film and writing projects. But a few years later, we suddenly found ourselves living on opposite sides of the country—she with her husband and two-month old baby in California, and I in New York, about to be married.

When I became pregnant, I felt isolated in my new city and anxious in my new condition. The two people I needed the most were my mother and Joan. But unfortunately, my mother had been dead for thirteen years, and Joan was on another coast. Long distance phone service was an extravagant luxury for me back then, and even when I did splurge I seemed to be too busy or too sleepy to experience the kind of closeness I really needed. So I turned to the parenting books I'd bought but never opened.

Joan had warned me to touch them only with lead-lined gloves. "Don't let them sink into you. They'll trivialize you. They want mothers to think that all the deep turmoil they're going through is insignificant, when it's really the heart of the whole human predicament.

"I mean, really—if engineers had to read this sort of condescending glop that dismissed all their 'silly' design problems with some cutesy list of *Do's and Don'ts*, they'd be jumping off bridges instead of building them."

There was always a grain of truth in Joan's conspiracy theories but that wasn't why my books were still in mint condition. It was because I'd been afraid to find out more than I wanted to know about childbirth. But wait—couldn't a *crumb* of sympathy be wedged in somewhere between the gory details and finger-pointing advice? Come on, Joan!

Well, not only did that crumb evade me, but most of the books seemed to be talking to some generic woman with generic concerns, offering one-size-fits-all advice.

I imagined I'd find far more comfort in asking Joan to write me about what she'd been through during her three pregnancies. She had two grown children and now a baby. I wanted to hear her singularly interesting, often wacky, and always compassionate take on things.

Before I moved to New York, Joan and I had enjoyed a long and fruitful history of complaining to each other. Of course, some people would have said, "Stop your belly-aching! Get on with it!" But belly-aching can be the first step toward change, can't it? If our forebears had politely swallowed their umbrage, there would have been no Revolutionary War, no United States and no Constitution to protect our rights to, well, among other things, belly-ache!

We felt that sometimes you had to muck through the bad to unearth the good. But as soon as Joan gave birth to Graham, there was no more kvetching between us. In fact, pretty soon there were no phone calls at all. She was drifting so far out into her isolated, organic world, I almost didn't know her anymore! She seemed so depressed, overwhelmed, and alienated I wondered if she belonged at the Betty Ford Clinic.

But where did I belong I had to ask myself. Certainly not here on planet earth where a normal mother wouldn't act or think the way I did! Despite our apparent polarities, Joan and I were both in the same boat, even if it would take us eight more years to recognize this. We were both plagued with feelings of self-doubt, shame, and alienation, as we struggled to claim individual answers from a sea of competing expectations, pressures, guilt, fears, and "good" advice. A sea of choices unknown to our more constrained and doctrinaire ancestors. This new freedom to personalize our mothering felt both wonderful and terrifying. Especially when it came to untangling the double bind of cultural contradictions!

If you put your child in daycare, you're abnegating your responsibility. If you keep her at home, you're depriving her of social experiences.

If you give in to him, you'll spoil him. If you don't play with him enough, he'll grow up sociopathic.

The Doublespeak of Big Mother.

Self-doubt oozed from underneath every parenting choice we made, as if someone somewhere, either alive or in a book were always judging us. But most of all, we were judging ourselves.

Eventually, after almost a decade of estrangement, Joan and I stumbled onto our new common ground. Apparently, all this parenting turmoil erupted from the same source: that deep and pervasive arch-conflict between what we thought we *should* be and who we really were. Underneath our disparate external dilemmas was a deeper and more universal challenge. The parenthood/personhood gap.

In spite of the 3,000 miles longitude and 180 degrees attitude that separated us, there was hope. We'd both taken a detour off the superhighway of convention to bounce down the potholed frontage road of individuation. Could there be asylum for the parentally-incorrect?

Maybe all of us really do want the same thing. And maybe we all want it because we *are* so different. Married parents, single parents, adoptive parents, grandparent guardians, older, younger, blind, gay, poor, rich, Asian, Apache, polygamist, circus folk and everything in between. Each one of us is an individual.

It took King Arthur's most dedicated knight to discover what a woman really wants. And that was, of course, to have her own way. Maybe mothers need it most of all. But who can have her own way until she knows her own way? I know for me, it took a lot of trying on and weeding out what didn't fit before I found what did.

Writing this book helped Joan and I see our own struggles, each other, and other people with more compassion. We hope *Motherhood Confidential* will help inspire other mothers to honor their own growth as much as they do their children's, and to find and embrace their own unique answers in their continuing quests for self-acceptance.

FETAL ATTRACTION

(or The Thing That Lived Inside Me)

in which Linda comes to terms with coming to term...

"It happened toooo me and it can happen to YOU-HOOooo—
For Godsakes Linda! Mary's six months pregnant and she can
shimmy lower than you!" Joan's singing Mary and me through
a dress rehearsal for our show-stopping Supremes number, the
Grand Finale for my "fertility party."

"Mary's gonna collapse trying to make you happy!" I choke
out my best noxious whine at Joan's evil Diana Ross.

"I've had about enough of your backsass, Flo. If you would
just emote a little, maybe she wouldn't have to act for the both
of you." Joan uncinches her four-inch wide patent leather belt
and snaps it like a bullwhip. "Mary, point to your belly on
'meeeee,' yeah. Good. Make it real obvious. And then gesture
over at Linda on *'you-hoooo,'* right!"

No one but Joan would have the guts or the gift to turn
the song "The Happening" into a fertility ritual. I think about
how much I adore her. Of course, that doesn't mean I go out
of my way to encourage her. Her red wig is ratted high enough
to shock John Waters. Her arms pantomime what appears to
be a stake through her heart. Swirling on stiletto heels she
mimes shooting Mary who slithers sensuously to the floor right
on cue. *"One day you're up!"* She's shooting me now. *"Next
day you're dow-oo-own!"* Mary writhes back up and I begin my

descent. If I could only look more sexy than stupid.

"Linda, if you can't ramp it up, Mary's going to be my one-woman back-up group!"

"Ouch."

It's Mary.

"She's gone into labor because of you!" I wail.

"No, it's this clip-on bow." Mary is struggling to free herself. "It snapped open into my brain."

The gigantic pink bow that apparently kept her bouffant wig from achieving lift-off looks like a padded bra ravaged by weasels. I ease it out from between the brunette layers armored solid with hairspray.

"John and I won't be back from Utah till the day of the ceremony, but I'm going to have everything set up before we leave."

"Oh, you don't have to do that." *Oh God. The ceremony?* Joan seemed intent on turning this nutty party into a sacrosanct affair. I'd tried to talk her out of it a couple of times. But with characteristic grandiosity she'd insisted this "gyna-fête" was important for "everyone!" Well, you can't argue with omniscience. So Joan would be racing back to the party from another opening of her independent film "Split," this time in her boyfriend John's hometown, Salt Lake City. I had a hard time imagining what a bunch of Latter Day Saints would make of Joan's sci-fi-comedy cult thriller.

"I think the fertility party will be good for John. I want to expose him to all that commitment energy. I know if I just keep at him I can wear him down." Unfortunately, Joan had moved in with the world's sweetest and singlest guy. Never mind all the women fragged by disappointment and all the brow-beaten but unrepentant men who'd gone before, *she* was going to change him.

They had spent their first date at my father's funeral. Not an auspicious beginning. That had been a few months ago.

Ever since then, my plan to have a baby had carried some sadness with it. Neither of my parents would ever meet their grandchild. But Joan said it was all the more reason to reinforce my connection to the life-giving forces of nature. She was probably right.

Mary pried the wig off her head, and I peeled off my sweaty boots, both of us trying to distract the Nazi choreographer. As much fun as I was having, I felt the urge to get home. I'd recently given up the stress of an independent rehabilitation counseling business for a mindless part-time waitress job, so I'd have more time to work on my novel. And, feeling unusually wide awake for such a late hour, that's exactly what I wanted to do. So I slipped on my sandals. Staring at Mary's bare feet, I urged her with a nod to do the same when I remembered we were in her house.

"See, I have a plan," Joan continued. "I *ease* John up the evolutionary ladder of commitment. You don't wanna start with a pet like a dog. Even a cat is too much too soon. That's clear. You start with the plant kingdom. Taking care of something that makes its own food and doesn't move. Not an inside plant. I got us a geranium. For the porch. You almost can't kill those."

"Isn't that going to take a few million years?" Mary asked.

"Oh. Yeah. Maybe it will. I don't get it. What's the big damn deal? It's like men think that marriage will change them into a legless life form or— "

"Or their dads," Mary finished matter-of-factly, plunging us into awkward contemplation. Normally I enjoyed awkward contemplation. But I knew if I left right away I could squeeze in that writing time. So I just blurted, "Gotta go!" and fled in a whoosh of costume-tossing and spilled liquor.

Driving home through the wet Berkeley streets, I began to feel extremely nervous. My plan to have a baby on my own before I got too old had seemed perfectly logical over the past few months. Why should I let all the fuss and bother of a relationship get between me and motherhood? Just do what had to be done: jot down a few healthy prospects on a *To-Do* List, stock up on the vodka, and brace myself for an action-packed ovulation. No dating required, just Instant Baby! But now that I was involving *The Goddess* and Joan's corny—but often surprisingly effective—do-your-own-voodoo, abstract theory seemed to be sliding towards practice. My uncertainty wanted a word with me. I felt like calling Joan and letting her know. It wasn't only *men* who felt afraid!

Personhood and parenthood. Did they always automatically merge smoothly together in a woman's life as they had for Joan? Was it really only for men that they were as volatile a mix as matter and anti-matter? Back in the good old days of last week, I was still in the Vague Notion stage of pre-motherhood, enjoying my own inner montage of tender Mary Cassatt moments. Little did I know that once I actually gave procreation the green light, reality and fantasy would begin careening toward an ugly smash-up. A freaky shiver ran down my spine. Was it only the fleeting discomfort of buyer's remorse, what Joan called "the natural outgassing of kinder-lust?" Or could it be—an actual *qualm?*

Well, I'd put off motherhood for forty years, so—sure, I didn't know too much about taking care of babies. But I had owned a tiny baby parakeet once named Jean Paul. Okay, he didn't need much nurturing. But come on, anybody could figure out the basics, couldn't they?

So what did a baby really need? Well, first off—a place to live, of course. I had that. It was a ten by ten room I rented from a friend, but I'd been told a baby fit nicely into a dresser drawer. Now what else? A father. Check! I was working on that. But there was one more thing, wasn't there? What was it—oh yeah, a mother. I guess he'd be needing one of those, too!

It was becoming all too obvious how blissfully and nightmarishly ignorant I was. But still, some of my best friends were mothers. Like Joan!

Joan loved being a mother. Even the single mother of two teenagers, working three jobs to keep a roof over their heads. Even those times when she felt she'd been a total failure—she still loved it. That gave me hope. After all, I couldn't imagine I was that different from Joan. We were two peas in a pod.

Both aspiring writers and actresses, we loved the same music, movies and Existentialists. In fact, the first time we met we were wearing the same outfit: tight blue skirt, white Ivy League blouse and wide striped necktie. So certainly, if my eccentric friend could handle motherhood, so could I.

Fortunately or unfortunately, my well-laid plans for pregnancy without partnership didn't pan out. I guess I didn't have the stomach—and probably wasn't the type—to just fling myself into the arms of the first guy on my *To-Do* List. Surrendering to fate seemed a lot less scary.

While pregnancy was still an abstract goal for me and a blurry teenage memory for Joan, we had the good fortune to observe, like stealthy bird-watchers, our friend Mary going through this strange metamorphosis in her natural habitat.

It was both revelation and riddle.

Mary's husband, Robb, loved to refer to the fetus as Rover. Joan was offended by this—really offended—in a sort of militant Victorian way. I wondered how a woman who makes jokes about the Vagina Stigmata in her comedy routine could be offended by Rover, but geez, it must have really pushed some button.

As I saw it, Robb was just trying to maintain a little distance as he eased into that terrifying role of father. But Joan insisted it was "so irreverent!" (until two year later when she began complaining about carrying *Zoltan, The Usurper*—a different matter altogether).

Of course, Mary had her own cryptic term of endearment.

"This baby" was all she called it. Never *my* baby. Always *this* baby. She'd say things like, "When I eat a piece of cheese, carrying around this baby doesn't make me feel as sick."

It seemed so impersonal and always made me laugh. Didn't pregnant mothers struggle to imagine their babies' faces and thrill to hear their little hearts thumping through the stethoscope? Wasn't there an innate drive to identify this mystery person, so inseparable and yet so foreign?

Being around Mary was like looking out from inside the TV, watching real people live. Her experience of motherhood was tangible and finite. Mine seemed so ethereal, a flickering mirage on the distant horizon. But as I plodded onward toward the Promised Land of Parenthood, something zoomed past me at the speed of light, sending me into a tailspin. It was Joan overtaking me on the inside with her whirlwind marriage to a mystery man. Like a bat out of Hell. It had been John's sudden death that catapulted her from her dismal bat retreat into that drive-by wedding in Las Vegas.

As uncertain as I was about her recovery from grief, and as little as I knew about this Thom guy, she seemed genuinely thrilled to be his wife. Seeing her so happy made it hard for me to give a damn if her happiness were unhealthy, fake, or possibly drug-induced. And it wasn't long before a baby was on the way. Maybe grief had boomeranged into baby fever, but if anyone had the experience, warmth and energy necessary for a re-run of motherhood, it was Joan. Funny how my close friends' pregnancies, so tangible and concrete, had made the idea that it could ever happen to me even more unreal.

But who knew? Two years after Joan it was my turn. I was over-ripe with maternal lust when I met Brian, and I fell like a fig in Autumn. What really solidified our relationship, though, was my resistance to settling down.

I wasn't exactly a gypsy—more of a slow moving transient. I loved the idea of spending a few years in a wonderful city and then moving on to explore another one. Even though a big part of me longed to settle down, the idea frightened me. It was too much like the life my mother had wanted me to have.

The whole reason she'd always discouraged my creative urges was not to hurt me, but to keep me focused on my Future of Safety, Stability and Security. For my refugee immigrant mother, security wasn't everything—it was the only thing. And I could understand that. But it was one of the few things in life I wasn't very interested in, especially if it meant sacrificing too much to get it.

My mother had been traumatized enough when I'd announced my decision to become a professional actress back in my late twenties. But she would have died if she'd lived long enough to see me at forty—still unanchored, working at part-time "nowhere" jobs and "throwing my life away" on the dream of becoming a published writer instead of running a good middle class home. Oddly enough, it was that vagrancy she would have so lamented that led to the fulfillment of the first step in the realization of her plan for my life—a stable marriage.

I'd met Brian through a blind date Mary had set up. He was an old boyfriend of hers and had flown out from New York to visit her and Robb, and meet the new baby. I'd been house-sitting in Oakland and needed a place to live. Brian had a rent-controlled apartment on Manhattan's Lower Eastside. It was a match made in heaven. He still sometimes thinks I moved there for his apartment and not for him. But believe me, I moved there because I wanted to get to know him.

And it was in that beautiful city that I did. Brian and I often went to Off-Off Broadway theatre, free concerts, interesting but cheap restaurants, or else just walked and walked. It was the kind of life I'd always dreamed of having.

Brian was open to having kids. I'd made sure of that. I was the baby-boomer stereotype, a forty-two-year-old woman who, because of my age, had run out of time to hem and haw. We never sat down and made the decision to actually try and have a baby, but we imagined it would be wonderful if it happened. And eight months later, it did.

We were more thrilled than we'd imagined we could be. Maybe I'd never have the three children I'd pictured in my dreams, but I was really truly going to have at least one.

In just a few hours, though, the sanguine song of bluebirds was drowned out by a horror movie score. I was suddenly filled with absolute terror over the idea of giving birth. Even more frightening, but harder to admit, was the prospect that my life would completely change after this baby was born, like a dungeon door slamming shut above my head. No more concerts or moonlit walks—just wailing, diapers and vomit.

But I had no time to fret about that apocalyptic future. The present was too busy disemboweling me. I felt like the "Alien" had invaded my body. I was glad I'd seen the movie because I was able to give a visual image to what I was experiencing. Still, I knew this was not what I was *supposed* to be feeling.

I had no sentimental feelings for this creature inside me. I couldn't relate to it. I couldn't picture it. I couldn't even conceive of it. (Well, I suppose I had done that—but only at the biochemical level.) I knew I was supposed to love It, but It obviously hated me. And the evidence seemed to support my theory that this thing wasn't human.

For one, it didn't make me feel sick in a way I was used to. In my experience, human beings are able to nauseate each other for all sorts of reasons. But if a person feels nauseous when the perpetrator isn't in sight, it's usually from a stomach-churning memory of their pain-racked history together.

I had no history with this mammal gestating inside my belly. In a way, it felt more like a bacterial infection. That was at least something I'd experienced before, but it wasn't the sort of "growth" I'd hoped motherhood had in store for me. And even though I'd seen first hand how the healing power of a friendly nickname had worked for Mary and Robb, I wondered if "Cowpox" or "Fungusboy" could really ease the antipathy of host toward parasite.

There were actually women (or so I'd heard) who lovingly played classical music tapes or read children's literature to their fetuses. The only thing I wanted to say to mine was, "Who are you and what do you want?" For the first time in my life I felt afraid of my own emotions. I figured the truth about my maternal angst should go no farther than the privacy of my own obviously twisted mind. Something was terribly wrong with me. Was it a symptom of my exposure to the Me Generation? Was it a character flaw? Or could this be a foreshadowing of family dysfunction to come?

I finally allowed myself to call Joan. I was a little intimidated by Joan's *born-to-mother* attitude, but she was the world's greatest empathizer. Even if my sub-maternal feelings surprised her, at least she wouldn't judge me. So I reached out. But to my bewilderment, that phone call made me feel worse. I almost wondered if I'd dialed the wrong number.

The Joan I knew back in California was, well... I've heard other "straight" women use this description for particularly special friends: "If only I were a lesbian! Darn it! She'd definitely be the one for me!"

Joan had the most expansive and kookiest mind—as if Kierkegaard's and Scooby Doo's synapses were constantly firing off each other, and a melodious, all-knowing laugh that, if only everyone in the world could hear it, might make us all go hysterical at once and bring about world peace.

Yet now, when I tried talking with her on the phone, it was no longer the Joan I'd once known with the quick mind and caustic wit. Though her kind but disjointed words were meant to comfort me, I only heard her thin, strained voice—unsteady, often fading, and full of frustration. I became exhausted myself as she tried to talk between, around, and seemingly from underneath the demands of her colicky baby.

After a few more attempts I gave up trying and said goodbye with a whimpered plea to "write me about what's going on if you get a chance." I was obviously on my own. Brian tried to listen, but I couldn't expect him to get it. It was up to me to fix my own maternal deficit disorder.

Where, oh where, had my tender yearnings gone? Was there anyone else in the world who felt like me, or should I be shot on sight? Mary's mild indifference seemed Madonna-like compared to my sudden urge to chew off my own foot like a trapped animal.

After ten weeks of nausea, I had a miscarriage. And yes, even with all those days and nights of anguish, it was a huge loss. It was, of course, also a relief. I wondered for a moment if I'd been punished for not wanting the baby enough. Nonsense. The God I believed in didn't work that way. Still, as I grieved for the baby, I tried not to enjoy my reprieve from motherhood too much. It was beginning to dawn on me that loving a baby and being a mother were two very distinct ideas in my mind. I had wanted that child, and I still wanted one. But I was afraid of being a mother.

After a miserable afternoon at the clinic for my D and C, Brian and I went out for dinner and I ate all kinds of spicy food I hadn't been able to stomach during the weeks before. If nothing else, my life was familiar again. And my own.

Five months after my miscarriage, I became pregnant again. I thanked God and was much more grateful than I'd been before, even though it was harder than the first time to picture myself carrying a fetus nine months and actually giving birth.

Having a miscarriage was a lot more real. In fact, after thirty long years of menstrual periods, all I could really imagine coming from that part of my body was excessive monthly bleeding and cramps.

Again, I was unsure if I had done the right thing. But to make matters worse, this time I was far more in touch with the Reluctant Mother Within.

I reminded myself I really liked kids and how I'd always wanted to have one, how good it had felt to hold my friends' infants—even *the tax advantages!* But I was still terrified to lose the life Brian and I had become used to together.

Couldn't I just saw a neat little hole in my life into which this baby would snugly fit? No, the surrounding floor would fall away in no time, leaving only a tiny cradle and a shrieking woman swinging from its rockers.

Then, in what seemed to be payback for my lack of fetal attraction, the incubus took revenge. Not satisfied with the subjugation of my bodily functions, X The Unborn mounted a campaign to plunder my all-important social life. The only thing I wanted at the end of each day was to sleep or be by myself so I could feel sick without any outside stimulation around to make it worse.

Everyone tried to help. "At least it's all worth it," they told me. "Once it's over you'll have a beautiful baby." Oh, really? Let me see if I have it right. After nine dreadful months Fungusboy will somehow turn into a pudgy Portobello? No. I couldn't picture it. My Mary Cassatt dream had become a Brueghel nightmare.

I looked forward to the sonogram though, hoping that seeing it and finding out the baby's sex might help me feel more connected. But when I found out the baby was a boy, I could relate even less to my experience.

How could a girl have a boy? I only seemed able to imagine a smaller version or myself, like a Matreyoshka doll, that Russian painted egg within an egg within an egg. How could a boy, who would someday grow into a man, actually be inside my womanly belly? On top of it, yes. But inside it? I couldn't fathom it.

It seemed I was on the verge of losing myself forever. Maybe I already had. In desperation, I picked up the phone to call Joan and then, coming back to my senses, slammed it down. I had to face the truth. Joan simply had no time left over for me. I'd been dumped like so much chozzerai to make way for the Needy One. What made me even more miserable was thinking that soon I'd have no time for her, either. As close as we'd been, as deeply as we understood each other, maternity was sentencing us to separate cells in a child-dominated oblivion.

Sometimes I tried to picture Joan's sparkling face, but all I could see were puffy eyelids, the bags underneath extending down to her chin, the dead eyes lost behind clumps of mangled, oil-soaked hair, as if she'd fallen into a pit mine of lithium. And why? All because she'd had a baby. *Because she was a mom.* And—oh no, say it isn't so—I was going to become one too.

The universe's greatest gift, a baby, had been given to me, and it was even what I had wanted—but it was all coming down to obsessive thoughts over my future deprivation. Would Joan ever be close to me again? Would my husband and I ever have a moment alone? And what woke me up in a cold sweat at night— would I never again go out for margaritas with the girls?

As all my life forces deserted me to serve the zygote, I recognized the problem. I just hadn't had enough practice being this unselfish. It wasn't coming easily, either. Even though I believed in Martin Buber's utopian philosophy of I and Thou, for me the *I* had more often than not come first. After living in a Me-topia all my life, how would I ever adapt to this new and frightening You-topia?

And the real sacrifices were yet to come. My body's little dictator hadn't even been born yet. Good God! That which does not kill us—can turn us into sniveling crybabies!

What a self-centered brat I was. That's all I kept telling myself.

GHOST OF
PREGNANCY PAST

(or True Crimes of a Haunted Housewife)

in which Joan experiences the wonder of mitosis...

Linda's baby-making plans had begun long before her hunt for a husband. Back when I first met her, Linda had already given up on the nuclear family idea, and resigned herself to having a baby the modern way. A one-night-stand with an old friend, or maybe two nights with a close acquaintance or—okay, if worse came to worst—as many stands as it took with the pizza delivery guy.

She started out as detached and cunning as a corporate head hunter, working methodically and unromantically to select her baby's father. I decided a fertility party might help things along.

Mary's back porch was pungent with jasmine that afternoon as twelve men and women stood awkwardly in a circle, chanting a rhyme about ripening fruit as we passed around white seeds and red wine. Then it was time for the potato ritual. "This is about redeeming the dark side," I announced, trying to unslur my speech. "It's very quick."

Linda rolled her eyes. I dealt the potatoes. "Just think about whatever's buried inside you that needs light. The potato loves the dark. So we give it our dark. Linda, don't just hold it! Rub it!"

I raised my potato. "Now heave! Throw all that repression and soaked up negativity away. Just take your potato, and let go!" I chucked mine with a grunted "Blessed Be," and it answered with a satisfying thud. Mary, who always went politely along with my homespun hocus pocus, sent hers with a lady-like underhand to rest in the azaleas—about two feet away. Linda wound up like Roger Clemens and pitched. After a moment of silence we heard it *THUNK-THUNK-THUNKING* down the neighbor's roof. The potatoes began to fly. Overcome by a liquored-up-mob-induced sentimentality, I sidled up next to Linda.

"Children are the answer," I pontificated as veteran mother to eager initiate. A few of us did wind up pregnant after that party, but not Linda. It took a while for the spell to work on me. Another funeral, a wedding, a year that seemed like five. I never dreamed that blessing would curse my relationship with Linda.

In the musical chairs of my new motherhood, Linda lost her special place in my life on the first round. Even though she never said anything, I knew she was a little shocked that a baby had come between us. But babies were only temporary, I told myself. They grow up into chubby spiders skittering across the floor in search of more and more independence. Pretty soon Linda and I would pick right up where we left off.

Still, I could understand why Linda missed the way it used to be. When I'd first met her, Tim and Tricia were already finishing high school. I had time for a best friend.

There was something we got out of our relationship—right from the very beginning—that we'd never found anywhere else. It was a synergy that launched a thousand projects and cushioned a thousand rejections. But it was more than that. It was a shared pool of empathy that reflected her inner turmoil to me and mine to her. That mutual transparency created a bond of understanding as powerful as gravity, worthy of a name and number on the heavy end of the periodic table. Lindallium.

When Linda went off to live on Bainbridge Island in Washington one year, I thought I was going to dry up and blow away without a dip in that mineral pond of validation. I didn't realize back then how solid our bonding really was—and would remain. She came home and we picked right up where we'd left off!

Before long our relationship was stable enough to go crazy in. (If you must have a nervous breakdown, it's really best to do it with a girlfriend.) Linda and I were both working in San Francisco's financial district when I had mine. My boyfriend, John, had just died. I'd been holding up pretty well—still temping, writing, and trying to make drunken comedy club crowds think I was funny.

After leaving my job at Rincon Center one day, I was hurrying across the streetcar tracks on Market to get to a murder mystery rehearsal in Union Square when suddenly I started weeping. Uncontrollably. I couldn't stop. And I couldn't move. I just stood there as if I were waiting for a thirty-ton shove to pitch me into the bay. Luckily nobody seemed to take any notice. I probably looked like just another down-sized middle manager freaking out on Market Street.

I stumbled to a pay phone and called Linda. We met at a bayside park. I sat next to a fountain, becoming its human twin, both of us immobile and overflowing. Linda just kept patting something that must have been my hand.

She visited me often during those next difficult months, but I couldn't talk. Clinical depression had shut everything down. Cold or hunger couldn't arouse a motor response. My psychiatrist assured me that a go-getter like myself would be back "swimming with the sharks in no time." He handed me a diagram of brain activity he'd scribbled on a post-it note. It looked like The Big Dipper.

"With depression," he pointed out, "all activity is concentrated in the threat perception area. What we wanna see are these areas lighting up, too," he emphasized by cartooning some fireworks above the narrow constellation. "The reasoning, the imagination. See, right now everything's being funneled through the Lizard Brain like an airport security checkpoint. So the whole system bogs down. That's what makes you feel like a wax figure. We call it The Madame Tussaud Syndrome." He laughed as if it were as common as chicken pox.

Well, my brain certainly did feel as restricted as a crime scene cordoned off for official homicide investigation. But that's because it was. Kojak was pacing around in there trying to find some way to nail me for John's murder. Oh, sure, the coroner said the cause of death was pernicious anemia. But wasn't that just Latin for somebody sucked the life out of him? I figured I belonged in a real wax museum between Jack the Ripper and Lizzy Borden for *nagging John to death*.

But one cannot feed on toxic guilt for long before the soul fights back. Of course it wasn't my fault! You can't actually kill someone with an overdose of marriage proposals. In fact, *he* was the Ratfink—for dying on me! I was back on track: focusing on my loss, my needs, my bloodlust! Feeling like a widow without officially being a widow had been far too mindscrambling. Repressed rage erupted in a Scarlet O'Hara vow of vengeance: "As God is my witness, I'll never go unmarried again!" The only way I could see to get over John's death was to replace him as soon as possible. But it had to be a man who was ready to commit to marriage, to family and to staying alive.

It wasn't long before both Linda and I had our eyes on the prize. It looked as if we might be getting married pretty soon. And even if it were to different people, it would be another phase of our lives we could share together.

With some gentle sheltered workshop time as Mary's babysitter and a high octane boost from Prozac I rocketed from bereaved to betrothed in seven months. Linda wasn't absolutely convinced I was dealing with my loss in the best of all possible ways by answering a personal ad. "You're in love with some guy you've never met? Couldn't he be writing to you from a work farm? You'd better make sure he's husband material."

But once she met him (shortly after I did), he who "looks like an axe-murderer, Joan!" became a "real mensch." She could see how deeply Thom respected me, how enthusiastically he raved about my talent, how rapidly he paid off my bench warrants. She was inspired to find her own Mr. Nice Guy.

The countdown was starting for Linda to get her first shot at motherhood—and for me to get my last. Soon we'd escape The Land of Ambivalent Boyfriends and enter the World of the Happily Married. With a couple of easy-going soul mates, the two high strung women could have it all. Work part-time, pursue writing, and raise children, too. Findhorn without the farming!

But I wasn't sure Linda really got the *children* part. She was very sensitive and fiercely protective of her emotional boundaries. How fast could she train a baby to be John Bradshaw?

But do any of us really know what we're in for when we decide to become parents? Is it even possible to plan rationally for this emotional, unpredictable, and right-brain-dominated journey? There's only so much a spread sheet can do. But maybe that's okay, as long as we have guts, imagination and the grace of inexperience.

My decision to have a child was easy. Maybe too easy. Thom was pro-parenthood. And I was no rookie. I already had two grown children. A third should be a snap. What was a mere twenty-one year gap between pregnancies? But as soon as I discovered I was indeed pregnant, I panicked and called Linda. By this time, she'd cancelled *Operation Man Breed* and was leaving everything up to fate. If she was jealous of me, it never showed.

But I couldn't put my feelings into words. It was more than shock or fear. It was as if I'd stepped into an elevator that only went down. And down. And down. My whole body seemed weighted with guilt. Guilt about how a baby would make me less available to my older kids who still needed me, and my mother who was beginning to need me more.

Suddenly I plunge to the floor below: *Notions, handbags, regret, self-blame,* until finally I'm hit with a sickly mix of relief and remorse—how much better off this child will be than my first two. My heart breaks for Tim and Tricia all over again.

On down into the past I plummet. Into the nightmare of my unwed teenage pregnancy. And beyond. Apparently this elevator doesn't stop at the basement or the parking garage. It just keeps sailing right down below sea level into the collective unconscious until I sink into Davey Jones' Shame Shack. And—funny—I feel right at home helping myself to the all-you-can-eat-smorgasbord of self-denial, where every pleasure comes with a side of guilt: *your happiness makes others suffer.* Had pregnancy turned me Catholic? I gulped down the painful thought of neglecting my children *again.* My head was spinning as I dialed Linda's number.

Despite my difficulty articulating those bizarre feelings, she thrilled to every stammering word. She was sure it was all a part of the glory of morning sickness. Beyond a doubt it proved to her my drunken fertility party prophecy was coming true! At that moment, however, I couldn't for the life of me remember what it was babies were "the answer" *to.* My own selfish desires? My willful neglect of responsibilities to my older kids and to my mother?

By the next day my emotional upheaval had subsided. Now I was sweating for a different reason. It was time to break the news about my pregnancy to Thom. We sat down to dinner at Harrah's in Tahoe where we'd just attended a friend's wedding. Our table had a panoramic view of the lake—the perfect setting if ever there was one.

Unfortunately, in my frenzy to make myself look unpregnantly alluring I had moussed my perm into a rigid hair helmet. But Thom wasn't looking at my face. He was wiggling his eyebrows like Groucho Marx and staring at my clingy low cut dress, the one I'd worn for our wedding six months before.

What was I worried about? Thom was a guy who sent twenty-page love letters, collected wind-up toys and cried over *Land Before Time!* This man had enough sentimental optimism to get us both through the shock of impending parenthood.

As I raised my glass of complementary champagne and made my announcement in a strained falsetto, I looked into his gentle brown eyes. This would be Thom's first child! Soon my fears would melt away in the warm glow of his euphoria.

But when I saw the horror behind his forced smile, I let him have it with a wallop of projection: "You said you wanted this!" I tried to stomp out, but my sequined spike heels kept snagging on the carpet.

Thom had a long struggle coming to terms with his new provider role. Over the next few weeks, we reeled between excitement and dread. Thom seemed perpetually on the verge of going out for that fateful pack of cigarettes.

I realized he was buckling under the strain when I asked him to pick me up some animal cookies on his way home—for perhaps the hundredth time. In his usual cheery computer programmer voice he told me what he really wanted to do was take the four-wheel drive to the store, ram it through the front window and mow down Aisle Seventeen.

I was too anxious to be comforting. This pregnancy was nothing like the first two. At nineteen, I was doing back walkovers. Now I could barely stand erect. My body seemed unable to respond to my wishes, as if I were a marionette and someone had cut all the strings. My diabetic mother could out-race me now, shuffling behind her walker. In the darker recesses of my black thoughts, I wondered if my own body was rebelling, refusing to make my selfish baby-making easy.

My ever-widening indentation on the bed looked like the fossil imprint of some devolved subhumanoid. It gave me the willies. Not because of what I looked like on the outside but because it seemed to suggest what I was becoming on the inside, a corpulent trough —swelling and devouring, selfishly fulfilling its own insatiable needs. Something dirty and irre-sponsible. And now that I wasn't employed, I had to fight to remember what my therapist said, that gestating was important work, too. Because now it seemed so obvious I was just a taker, mooching of my over-worked husband.

Had it only been eight weeks since I'd had a full-time job and six agents who filled my free time with comedy gigs, auditions and commercials? I no longer knew that person who was so energetic. Could an inert lump hold down a job? Or was I to become a deadbeat wife?

It was as if layers of me were falling away, and I wasn't sure there was any real substance underneath. Maybe after all these years of working on personal growth, I was really no more than a superficial outer shell thinly coating some hideous amorphous center.

I could imagine all the other pregnant women at the helm of power centers around the world—prosecuting, legislating, atom-smashing right up to the day their babies were born— while I sat catatonic in a dingy bathrobe, moaning over my mini-donuts in front of *TJ Hooker*.

But I'd never even liked *T J Hooker*. It was that embryonic enforcer within controlling me, pulling me off the main high-way and into the all-night diner of the vagrant soul. One moment I was imprisoned in my immobilized body, the next hovering above it in disgust. But I no longer felt I lived there.

Soon it became almost impossible to walk. A major set-back for me. Our little subdivision in Hercules was a typical bedroom community except for the miles of beautiful hiking trails. Acres of open space had been preserved from develop-ment by proximity to the old explosives plant that once ran this company town. I had loved walking down the tracks to the towering gates of rusting filigree, through which I would stare at those romantic old brick buildings crumbling gracefully into the weeds. Hiking would have to wait. My existence was becoming all Yin and no Yang, passively retreating into the space between bed and refrigerator.

There was so much of this new me I didn't like. It was as if my old self were standing impatiently beside this new invalid self—chiding and ribbing, embarrassed to be seen with her. And my new self wishing only to become invisible. The two of us mismatched, but somehow stuck with each other. Like the place I now called home, that drab and docile subdivision nes-tled in the ruins of a dynamite factory.

My little flicker of sentience dwindled down to an ember. And a powerful dream visited me in that twilight existence.

I was driving some kind of huge, black car. Not really shaped like a car at all, it looked more like a bizarre steam locomotive patched together out of old film projectors and espresso machines. Remnants of my past.

There was no room for a cab, so I just hung onto the out-side like an old-time engineer might do. Whatever was inside must have been under tremendous pressure. Thick soldered seams webbed the black metal—to keep it from exploding, I guess.

Its internal mechanisms were fussy and sensitive. Any small

disturbance could knock it out of whack, so it would often break down. When it stopped dead in the middle of a small town square, I had a feeling it was going to be difficult to fix.

Later, I found myself squeezed inside a nameless, shapeless, cream-colored compact—a ubiquitous bland Japanese model that didn't seem to belong to me. It was more of a public commute car. I felt neutered inside this streamlined pod that was just like everybody else's. I missed the idiosyncratic Loco Motive. That old engine had been my own creation, something I'd worked on myself and had with great effort managed to keep running. The new car seemed completely automatic. I was simply a passenger along for the ride.

The dream expressed my resistance. I wasn't ready to abandon the old Loco-motivated self—as unpredictable and explosive as that personality was?in order to blend in with the tranquil anonymity of family life as a domesticated engineer.

That certainly wasn't what Thom expected of me. But perhaps it was what I expected of myself. I was probably subconsciously worried that my sometimes excessive individuality might cause trouble, as it had when I'd been a mother the first time.

I'd always felt my first two children had left me because of my artistic mania. When I became obsessed with performing stand-up comedy, Tim and Tricia were seven and ten, and they probably felt they were taking a backseat to my personal ambition. At Christmas they left to visit their father a thousand miles away, and then politely called to tell me they weren't coming back.

They tried to spare my feelings. "Daddy's lonely," they explained. The first year I was certain they'd come home any day. The second year I grieved. When they finally came back, the shockwave of guilt and gratitude should have turned me into June Cleaver. It didn't, but my children pretended to notice vast improvement.

My odd transportation dream had to be about releasing anxiety from the past. The fear of this baby taking a backseat, too. But I wasn't living in a flophouse hotel anymore, hawking perogies on the street corner so I could commit my crimes of obsession. Only in memory would I relive the halcyon days of stand-up life—the glory of emceeing an exotic male strip show, the privilege of opening for Phil The Phartman, or the thrill of fleeing a horde of boozed-up bikers riled by my pithy social satire. That was all ancient history.

The only danger I faced or posed was that of dissolving unnoticed into the void. In my new role as incapacitated hausfrau I was as inoffensive and conforming as our little grey condo. But the dream images stayed with me until I came out of my coma. In my eighth month it happened. I could move. Without moaning.

I shed my crusty pupa—ready now to indulge in the sugary birth announcements and bunny-infested baby books I'd missed out on with my first two children. I'd never had any disposable income before I married Thom. Now that I did, I was disposing of it as quickly as possible.

Things were going to be different with this pregnancy! Timothy had been born out of wedlock, Tricia just barely in. But the third time would be the charm! Ahhh—to savor the sweetness of that word, Congratulations! What an improvement over the old, "Shit, what are you gonna do now?"

It was a thrill when at last I had the strength to take a real bonafide walk. A breeze rustled the eucalyptus that day as I followed the tracks by the shoreline past the park that disguised a sewage treatment plant. Here the road curved, and as I waited to cross it I saw my pregnant shadow loom across two lanes. A car ran over it as if it weren't there.

Staring at my distorted shadow, I was embarrassed by the grotesque exaggeration of my condition. But it went beyond embarrassment—there was something repugnant about it. I shuddered as an avalanche of dread crashed through me. And then out of the blue I was gripped by the realization that I should be murdered. Not *would* be or *could* be—but *should* be murdered. I was almost resigned to it. As if I had it coming.

I was no longer an adult. I had been yanked back in time. Or perhaps the past had caught up with me because suddenly I was that unmarried pregnant fifteen-year old girl all over again, carrying a shame so colossal it cried out for any punishment that could obliterate it. Even murder.

My shadow was frozen on the road. I knew then that I would be run down by some phantom-driven muscle car. Naturally. That was the cheap tawdry end I deserved.

I managed to step back from the road, but I couldn't step out of that death scene. It was as if I'd fallen through a rabbit hole into a 50's teen crime movie, and suddenly I saw myself lying in the street, listening to the screeching tires of a hit-and-run Torino. My final conscious act would be to stare up from the blood-soaked asphalt at the craggy lieutenant who'd be grinding out a cigarette with the toe of his wingtip beside my twisted carcass. "Kids having kids," he would spit, waving my body bag into the meat wagon.

Turning from the nightmare, I began to shuffle back along the tracks. But the horror would not stay behind. A clingy oppressive presence seemed to be shadowing me. Like a huge and sinister Jiminy Cricket. Zippity-doo-dah-*DIE!*

Twenty-five years after that pregnancy, my old shame had re-emerged. Now that I was married to a good man, leading a life that was safe and secure, it wanted its old room back.

From then on, for almost two years, my guardian hovered over me, silently waiting until I experienced any form of sensual pleasure. Then it would spring to life, contaminating every joy with its malignance.

Breastfeeding became a morbid blend of intimacy and self-loathing. Even the simplest satisfaction—a full stomach or sunshine on my skin—was replaced by an abysmal feeling of doom. This golem had come shambling back into my life, driven by a re-animated sense of Puritanical duty, poisoning all self-gratification to keep me from "getting into trouble" again, apparently unaware I already had.

This was the kind of X-File phenomenon that wasn't easy to explain to Thom or Linda, but I tried. They listened politely and nodded as they would to Jimmy Stewart describing his giant invisible rabbit.

After I stopped nursing, that Hell-spawned Harvey finally slithered back into hibernation. But it had helped me understand some things. Like why I'd always pushed myself to work seven days a week. I was scared to relax! Afraid to let myself fully experience joy. The Pleasure Police were on a continuous stake-out in my head.

Now it also made sense to me why I'd been so reluctant to tell my mother I was going to have another baby. I was four months along before I could face it.

Logically, I knew she'd be thrilled. But logic was no match for terror. Every time I thought of telling her, I could only feel disgust for the words I'd barely been able to whisper twenty-five years before. How could I even say that word, *pregnant,* out loud to her? It was a profanity.

My pregnancy wasn't a beautiful thing to shout about. It was just a dirty secret that proved I'd been a bad girl. *A selfish tramp who didn't care about the pain she caused others!* Or so harped the litany from my internal *all-self-blame-all-the-time* station.

There I was at forty, a grown-up married woman with two adult children and years of therapy behind me, unable to tell my mother I was pregnant. So Thom and I went to see her together. I giggled nervously as I gripped his hand in my sweaty palm. My voice sounded strangely high as I blurted out that *Thom was going to have a baby.*

There! Nothing sordid about that! It was just a wonderful thing happening to a wonderful guy! My mother laughed and clapped her hands. She embraced me with more strength than I thought she had in that seventy-eight-year old body. In her arms I felt wholesome and good and loved.

But there was still something haunting me. The Ghost of Friendship Past. As my due date neared I thought of Linda, and realized I hadn't been any kind of friend to her over the past few months. But I could make up for it now that I was ambulatory again.

I was already working on a comedy roast for her Going Away to New York Party. Yet, even then during that brief hiatus of confidence I was beginning to wonder if it would ever be the same between us. I was coming unmoored from our friendship. This time it was me going off to an island, and I was never coming back.

THE OUGHTABEES MEET
THE WANNABEES

(or Unconventional Etiquette)

in which Linda gets a belly full...

For two people who'd seen eye to eye, shared the same dreams and finished each other's sentences, Joan and I were having a hard time adjusting to this uncomfortable gap in perspectives. Now that Joan was mother to an ever-squalling infant, I'd pretty much given up talking to her on the phone, but I had asked her to write me, and two years later she did. One single-space-typed thirty-page letter with so many stains and typos it was almost illegible.

What she wrote about her pregnancy puzzled me.... She'd been in so much pain, yet it seemed her greatest anguish was that she wasn't like "other pregnant women" who could work and gestate at the same time.

But we were both tired of grinding away at jobs we didn't like, and I thought she'd be grateful she had a husband to support her. What I wouldn't have given to be lounging at home now in my first trimester! But there was something about feeling *incapable of working* that gave her a sense of inferiority. Now *that* I could understand!

One day I realized that the world I was in was not the same one other people lived in. I seemed to be a prisoner behind The Nausea Curtain. It was as if everyone else existed at a higher rate of vibration. I watched them laughing, schmoozing, making movie deals while I stood there invisible. No longer functioning in that human range of vibration, I seemed to have plummeted to the level of mealworm.

Riding the subway to work during my first trimester, I felt like a whale on a skateboard. I had to brace my head against the cold window of the door just right so I could counterbalance the twisting and turning of my insides with that of the train.

On one such morning, as I leaned against the door as if to keep some phantom hanging onto the window from getting in, we shrieked to a stop at 23rd Street Station. As I moved to let a few passengers by, I watched an attractive young man across from me offer his seat to a woman who must have been nine months pregnant. At that moment I wished I'd had a large sign plastered across my chest: EXCUSE ME! HELLO! I'M PREGNANT TOO! Would I actually have to spew vomit to let these commuters know I felt like hell?

It dawned on me then that I'd have to wait at least five months for a seat, until I'd graduated to that supposedly blissful Ripe Demeter stage and probably wouldn't need one anymore!

I certainly developed empathy for people with "invisible" chronic diseases like arthritis or cancer. Unlike me, they had no reassurance their pain or nausea might actually end at some point. But their agony never showed. Well, maybe it showed, but it was probably misinterpreted by me and everyone else as despair over the dreaded project kick-off meeting. Those were people who needed big sandwich boards: I'VE GOT LESS THAN A YEAR TO LIVE, LET ME LIVE IT LIKE A THIRD TRIMESTER PREGNANT WOMAN! They were the ones I really felt for, maybe because I could never be that stoic.

My father had a favorite joke about an old Jewish man in prison. The old guy is weak with thirst and can't stop moaning and groaning. "Oy! Am I toisty! I am so toisty. Boy, I AM toisty!! I'm *soooooooo*—" He wails on and on and on until finally the warden down the hall can't stand it anymore and brings him a cup of water. The old man drinks it down with a great sigh of satisfaction. "Aaaah!" The warden grabs the cup and goes back down the hall to his post. And in the distance, "Oy, was I toisty! I was so toisty. Boy, I WAS *toisty! REALLY toisty!* I was *sooooo*—"

I think my father was poking fun at complainers, but that was never the way I looked at that story. I saw it as a parable about the natural urge to complain. I've always needed to vent, to cry out, to express turmoil, whether I'm in the middle of some deprivation, attack or trauma, or haunted by its memory.

Yet everyone suffers from society's Spartan mandate. As a pregnant woman in my first trimester I felt I was expected not only to hide my pain, but maybe even be *grateful* for it. And that's what made it so much worse.

I dragged myself onto the elevator in the Empire State Building one morning, heading up to the office, as an older man trailed behind me. The doors shut, and he and I were alone. I had just come from climbing the never-ending cement stairs in the steamy, smelly subway station as I did every day that summer, with my whole body squeamish, the lump in my middle starting to show.

"How ya feelin'?" The nice man smiled after a quick glance at my belly. "Ya doin' good?" I'm sure he thought everything was supposed to be good for me then—what with my bringing a new life into the world and all. But I couldn't lie. If only I'd smiled back and said something upbeat, maybe I would have even convinced myself. We would have had a nice little interchange to start our day. A real New York moment. Right then I wished I had Joan's black belt in B.S. She could always come up with a snappy excuse, fib or retort. My inability to bend the truth even a little often annoyed her.

"It's not lying," she would explain. "You reframe. Like in acting." Easy for her to say. I wasn't sure I could reframe my feelings—or hide them or ignore them if my life depended on it.

So I was honest, "Well, actually, I'm not feeling so good right now." The man nodded and gave a compassionate "Oh," but then his smile disappeared and he quickly glanced away. What had I expected? That he would flop down on the floor for a mini-Esalen session to Gestalt out all my deepest pain and fear? No, we were in New York after all, so instead the elevator became echoingly silent. He got off on the fifteenth floor with a quick relieved wave back to me. I felt bad for him all the way up.

Why had I set myself up to feel worse than I already did? All of a sudden I could hear the answer—not in my own voice, but in a lilting Texarcana accent: "Because you're just a bucketful of hormonal sludge, Honey!" It was the voice of Chinette Sleazak.

Chinette would have known just how to help me. And she wouldn't tell me to reframe anything! She was shockingly honest. A girl after my own heart! She wasn't afraid of what anybody thought of her. After all, she had twelve children of her own, each from a different father. And even though she was too busy watching funny-car races to spend one minute of time with any of her "babies," they all were happy and secure.

She was honest. She was loving. And she was imaginary. So you didn't have to fly three thousand miles to be with her.

Chinette was one of Joan's alter egos who'd show up at parties in her tight gold lamé pants and inch-thick make-up. She seemed to have a certain wisdom Joan could only access when she was under that mass of ratted hair.

If only Chinette had stepped onto that elevator then, slicing the air with her salmon blush nails like a drunken priest giving benediction. "Honey, you're entitled to all the crappy feelings you want! You're pregnant, damnit!"

I shared Chinette's inability to repress anything, but not her immunity to self-criticism—the combination of which made her a force to be reckoned with.

I wondered then if Joan had ever resurrected Chinette while she was pregnant. Maybe if she'd just put on the big wig like a shaman puts on a deer's head, the messages would have come to her, something like, "What's with all your macho bullpucky about some Pregnant Puritan Work Ethic? As soon as men can get pregnant, they'll call it a medical illness again! You're not macho, Sweetie—you're catatonic. Now, live up to it!"

But how could Joan ever have heard those words over the loud voices in her head spewing the edicts, indictments of Motherhood Yet-To-Be?

Imagining Chinette's refreshing perspective brought me some comfort, but I still wished I could have honestly said to that guy in the elevator that everything was wonderful. Even bored him to death with my tales of womanly fulfillment.

The worst part about feeling sick the first five months was having almost no joyous moments to share with the rest of humanity. And of course I wasn't any good at hiding all the bad feelings I was having.

I tried to tell Joan about the whole mess. "I feel like something's wrong with me. You know. It's that feeling again—that I just don't experience any of this like I'm supposed to."

"Oh, god, yes. I remember when I was lying in bed all those months."

"Right! I remember now. Did you ever—"

"Every minute! I felt so incredibly deficient as a human being till I met someone else who'd gone through the exact same thing."

"You met—"

"One other person—that's all it took. I wasn't a lazy scumbag or some worthless aberration of nature anymore."

"That's great," I said without feeling. Then I lashed out, "But I am! So what am *I* supposed to do? Lock myself up because nobody feels this way but me?"

"I'm sure there are other people who—"

"And what if there aren't?" I cut her off. "What if I *am* the only one who can't feel the right feelings and who's this devastated by all the judgments —what does that say about me?" I was being insensitive to her and I knew it. Her pregnancy had been a hundred times worse than mine but I didn't want to hear about it. I just wasn't in the mood to be in some kind of game show lightning round competition over our pregnancies. She would win hands down. So what did I want from her? I had no idea. What were we even talking about? All I knew was that she had no idea what it was like to feel this sick and *still be able to work.*

Joan was silent a moment. "This all says you're brave! Very brave. You—"

"Hey, I don't care! I never said bravery mattered to me. I said I'm a deviant!"

A pregnant pause. "Then maybe," she suddenly blurted out, "You should let your freak flag fly! Isn't that what Brian always says?"

Yeah, that was what Brian always said. It was his pre-emptive strike against my perpetual angst. But that wasn't what I needed now.

"You don't get it! That flag is flying! And I wanna burn it! I would like to just feel normal for once!" I tried to explain to Joan about the elevator event when the background bawling rose like a jet fighter taking off. Then came the dial tone. Our usual *adieu.*

Beyond the gnawing disappointment in myself, I felt that I was a disappointment to the whole world. A mother without joy is a failure. I also felt that I'd offended Joan, but I was way too tired and grouchy to call her back. Besides, her growing inaccessibility was starting to get me down.

The pregnant woman is supposed to be a sort of shimmering Persephone frolicking through the world tossing lavender bouquets, an icon of hope and delight, isn't she? Should I have been trying harder?

Hope and delight—that's what every baby and mothers' magazine tries to capture. *Or manufacture.* All you see on the covers are images of joy. Joy—or living courageously through tragedy. Could there possibly be something in-between?

It seemed to me that unless you're living in a decimated trailer park with eight foster children, your entire herd of milk goats wiped out, your problems are mere whiney complaints. I felt entitled to only two emotions: Selfless Joy and Martyrdom.

So what should I say when some anonymous man in an elevator asks me, "How ya feelin'?"

Which one do I choose?

1. Joy—*or at least mock joy*: "I feel great! Every day is a new experience!"

2. Martyrdom: "I feel great, even though my pancreas works about as well as the bottom of an old shoe! I am so excited. It will be fun to see how I'm going to support this baby now that my uninsured husband was just run over by the N-train! Every day is a beautiful day when they let me out of the women's prison to clean the toilets here. I can throw up any time I want!"

Everybody loves to see a pregnant woman. *See.* Not *hear.* The Glow! The Madonna-like placidity. The fecund fruit form that stirs ancestral memories of bounty and survival. But it was hard to be an icon.

I knew I couldn't do it. Chinette understood. I Am Pregnant Woman! Hear Me Roar! Sometimes in rage, sometimes in pain. Sometimes in utter and absolute confusion!

AU NATUREL

(or Battlefield: Birth)

in which Joan lets nature take its course...

What could be sexier than a husband in a surgical gown! That's what Linda and I thought the night we'd visited Mary and Robb in the hospital with their firstborn. Well, unless it was a man massaging his pregnant wife's tailbone.

When I was pregnant, it wasn't enough for me that Thom came to the birthing classes. I wanted more than his passive compliance. I wanted the romance of his eager participation. But Thom just couldn't see the sexiness of it all. Well, I was probably enthusiastic enough for two.

I'd had a wonderful natural birth with my second child, and I was ready to do it again. I thought women who had epidurals were cheating themselves of a peak experience, and women who had cesareans deserved my condolences. There was no greater ecstasy than a drug-free birth!

Perhaps because I fancied myself such a free thinker, I was blind to the judgment that lurked behind that attitude—the subtle criticism of any woman who chose a birthing method other than my "right" way. What I did notice, as my due date neared, was a huge sense of relief that at last my experience of gestation actually matched my own rather rigid expectations. I felt good, strong and prepared for the perfectly proper birth ahead.

It was a dark and stormy night when we arrived at Oakland's Summit Hospital with enough recording equipment, cable, and duct tape to launch our own satellite network. Thom kept me laughing as I began my confident laps around the maternity wing. Thirty-six hours later my fruitless labor was explained to me. "The baby's pushing at the wrong point."

In my exhausted stupor I wondered, is he trying to tunnel his way out? Doesn't he know there's a door? Now each contraction felt like a ghostly sailor banging against the hull of his sunken ship. To help "re-orient" the baby a small medical team strapped me upside down on some kind of medieval rack. Technology by the Marquis de Lamaze?

As I lay there like a frog awaiting dissection, the blood rushing to my head and the contractions engulfing me, I fought off the tears and tried to think logically.

Surely there could be some explanation for this turn of events that didn't involve human sacrifice. It was quite possible that the terror of being stranded on a stuck tilt-a-whirl was supposed to dwarf the pain of childbirth.

Still, it seemed more logical that any minute the doors would swing open and in would swagger a foppish obstetrical fiend, flinging off gloves and mask so that he could perform a *natural* delivery. But he must have been busy with another vivisection because he never showed.

I ended up facing something far worse. A bubbly nurse. "It didn't work," she chirped—the way a pert news anchor can make a plane crash sound fun. "Your contractions fell off. You might as well go home."

Thom had been staring out the window. Not because he was bored, but because for this wannabe storm-chaser, weather was the ultimate élan vital of the universe, explaining everything from itchy scalp to the national debt.

"It's the weather," he pronounced. "Your contractions follow the storm. When it was pouring you were fine. Now that it's subsided, nothing's happening."

Oh great, the baby wants rain. It can't be something easy like a ten-speed. No, it has to be an act of God. Well, God might be busy helping another customer, so I decided I'd better orient this baby myself. I spent the next hour in a Yoga posture I had learned—Gaping Cabbage or something. The contractions came back hard and fast. At last it was time to push.

I struggled to get into some position that could help me, but ended up on my back. Pain took control of my body, and I couldn't tell if I was bearing down or not. The encouraging chorus of "Push! C'mon, push!" was heartwarming, but not that compelling without a gun in my ribs. I could almost hear Scottie shouting back from the engine room. *"Captain, she canna stand the strain. Any more and she's like to blow!"*

I wished I could. My pain-o-meter, already beyond *Eternal Damnation,* was soaring past *Boyfriend-1977.* Wasn't my coach-*slash*-husband supposed to have a few tricks up his sleeve that he should be pulling out about now? Like yanking the camcorder off the tripod to deal a few solid blows to my skull?

Maybe if I stopped trying—just gave up—maybe I could passively endure the agony. Endurance was second nature to women, wasn't it? Maybe other women. All I could do was scream. That I did quite well. But it didn't ease my pain or help me deliver. If only I could scream myself into oblivion. Thom leaned over me and sobbed. I sobbed with him for a moment, then continued screaming until they told me I could stop. The birth had finally happened to us. I could hear thunder. The rain was coming down in sheets.

As the nurses tidied me up, I wondered why it had never occurred to me to bellow out, "Epidural!" "Morphine!" or "Buckshot!" Was I afraid to fail? Ashamed I couldn't do what I was "supposed to?" It was easy for me to encourage other people to resist the tyranny of the *shoulds*, but hard to do it myself.

I lifted my heavy head to see Thom collapsed onto a nearby folding cot compact enough for space travel, his arms spilling out to either side like a scarecrow. He looked just like he did in our wedding photo, his face a gruesome anarchy of joy and terror like he'd just been reading a really funny letter bomb before it went off.

Our midwife, Nancy, leaned over and whispered in my ear, "You labored beautifully." I winced. *Loudly, maybe, but certainly not*—not what? Not good enough? Her kindness finally penetrated.

"Thank you." Clutching my little pointy-headed reason for living through that "peak" experience, I knew I was now a member of that legion of shell-shocked women who remember childbirth only in terrifying PTSD flashbacks. Whose approval had I so desperately needed that I was willing to twist a perfectly normal childbirth into a marathon of martyrdom? There was no one in my family. It certainly hadn't been Thom or Linda. Well, that only left Ye Olde Worst Enemy.

The Law of Natural Childbirth had somehow intruded itself into my shadowside *shoulds*. Right next to a few other dubious dogmas like Others Come First and Make Men Feel Superior, that dictated quietly but imperially on the dark side of my consciousness.

As I tapped the toes of this little creature, I felt I might be contaminating him. He was still free. Unfettered by the petty tyrannies of the psyche. If only I could make him immune to mine.

Then as the moon rose to shine into our third floor suite, Linda peeked in the door. I hadn't seen her in six months and yet she'd made the trip out to see me. I felt awkward. And I wasn't sure why. This was one of the most intimate and significant events of my life and she was my most intimate and significant friend. If she noticed my discomfort or was dealing with any of her own, it was hidden under the comic grandeur of her entrance.

"Oh Dahlink!" She hugged me, her silky brown hair brushing against my neck. The ice broke and I was swept up in her warmth, wishing she'd been with me in the delivery room. She would have been a good doula. She would have brought Whiskey! She would have plugged in a Doobie Brothers tape! And she would have been dancing around the room tipsy while I screamed my lungs out.

She glanced at the baby. "It's little." Linda wasn't baby-crazy. I liked that about her. All Women Must Adore Babies was one of those gnawing *shoulds* I just couldn't live up to. But I wondered how deep Linda's aversion ran. Someday, she, too, was going to have to diaper and burp and comfort. Nope. Linda was not a comforter or a nurturer. She was a motivator, a supporter. If only she could raise a baby by validating its needs instead of meeting them!

She wrenched her eyes from the suckling horror and gave me a big toothy grin. "Your hair has a kind of a wild sea breeze look. Did you have one of those water births?" I laughed, and she smiled at me with just the right amount of pity. But then she snatched the pity back for herself.

"I hope I still belong in your life ..."

Oh boy. The ol' switcheroo. Linda and I had a strange chemistry. If I was sad, it hurt her. If I was angry, it scared her. If I was happy, she might feel left out. She wouldn't hide it or sulk. Linda was no more capable of that than she was of repressing the feelings the rest of us smothered under etiquette, fear of reprisal or good old denial. Emotion felt, emotion expressed. The tables turned and whatever I was going through would have to wait while her feelings took center stage.

But Linda never held onto an emotion long enough to let it build up steam, so these episodes only lasted a few minutes.

It was just that today—this time—I wanted the empathy all for myself. But I nodded and made sympathy noises. When she hugged me I found myself once again wearing the stupid grin of the overly thanked, secretly fleeced sucker. Still, the payoff was worth it. Now her ebullience was crackling the air.

"Can we ring the buzzer for room service? You know they should have hot dog vendors up here!" I almost resented laughing because I wanted to be mad at her for turning my birth experience into her own melodrama.

Late that night, during a break in the incessant stream of hospital procedures I found myself alone with this soft little lump and I sank into a new universe of mutual gratification.

I melted with wonder. This was not a child I saw. Nor was it a baby. To identify it as flesh and bone was not even accurate. The word "human" seemed distant and narrow. That's when I realized why we call it "newborn." New Born. An adjective without a noun. In this unfinished state of being, it was unknowable. More a part of eternity than finitude. An epiphany held in the web of time and space.

Looking down at him, I was glad he was small. I could just bear his radiance. Any more of it and I would have probably gone mad like any mortal face to face with Pan. I wondered if I could make this being comfortable in my mundane world. Well, first I'd have to break the ice. I smiled at him and whispered three names.

The next morning I was surprised to discover that Thom had done the same thing. With both of us there had been a response to one name only.

Maybe it was the beginning of his story. The one who comes from the gray house. Born of the gray storm. With the courage to live between the black and the white. Graham.

DOGMA DRAGNET

(or Invasion of the Know-It-Alls)

in which Linda learns being pregnant means your body belongs to the world...

Now that I was pregnant I really missed the company and confidence of a close friend, but I hadn't been in New York long enough to make one. If only Joan or my mother could have been with me. Maybe things would have been a little easier.

Joan would have at least tried. She would have put a lot of effort into supporting my feelings, though she would've had to shout above the infant din. And my mother, while probably nagging a lot, would have staunchly defended me against all others. As it was, I had only my loving, but (through no fault of his own) non-female husband, so I had to reconcile the discord between my inner and outer realities pretty much alone.

Brian and I got married at New York City Hall when I was four and a half months' pregnant. Our reason for choosing that particular Wednesday in June was exceptionally unromantic. I had an appointment for a sonogram in the morning at Kaiser Clinic, and if we got married that same afternoon, I wouldn't have to lose more than one unpaid work day—I'd be able to kill two birds with one stone, as they say.

So I had the sonogram, and afterwards the nurse told us there was something on the baby's brain. I didn't know if I should play it down or worry myself sick.

Were Brian and I strong enough or mature enough to raise a child with a brain problem or one who could end up dying? *It could be just a shadow, they said. Don't be concerned.* They had to be cautious, though. So they would pay for me to go to Einstein Hospital in the Bronx to have another sonogram and be evaluated by experts. Unfortunately, I'd have to wait another two weeks to get in.

We got married that day in spite of it, and we both did a good job at convincing ourselves that whatever it was on the baby's brain was really nothing. By the afternoon, my nausea had let up a bit, so I was able to rather enjoy the whole experience—the 45-second ceremony, the hawkers outside City Hall shoving bouquets of flowers in our faces for us to buy the moment we walked out the door, the muggy June thunderstorm. Ahh yes, the Big Apple.

New Yorkers are either totally indifferent, or else get intimately involved with you in a moment's time. I felt fortunate to be living there the day I called for bus information to Einstein Hospital. It was similar to the experience I'd had one spring morning on a deserted sidewalk on my way to work, when some guy up ahead turned around and yelled out to me, "It's a beauty-full day! Don't ya think?"

I loved that man for connecting me to New York City and the world and every living thing in it. My phone conversation with the bus information clerk made me feel just the same way.

"Hi, can you tell me how to get from Second Avenue and East Twelfth to Einstein Hospital in the Bronx around one o'clock on Friday?" I asked.

"Hmmm, let's see, buses only stop at Einstein once in a while," he said, studying his schedule. "You know, sometimes they can really make you wait there. I've been to the clinic over at Einstein. And me—I'm a worrier. I don't like to wait at hospitals. It gives you more time to imagine things—I don't know, are you like that?"

"Well, yes, sometimes I am."

"You'll have to transfer at a stop in the middle—we won't be able to get around it—there's a coupla choices here, and I don't want you waiting at the transfer point long—it's a headache. But I hafta make sure you're not late, either."

"What?"

"Gimme a minute to look over these times here. *I don't want you to be late.*"

When our conversation ended, I nearly wept. *He* hadn't wanted *me* to be late. I'd lost my parents when I was in my thirties, but now I knew Manhattan bus information would always be there for me when I needed fatherly advice and caring words.

Earlier, I had telephoned friends and family to let them know I was married. I remember Joan squealing with glee, and we giggled happily and frothed about it for a minute before she had to get off the phone and take care of the little Caesar.

I didn't tell anyone about the spot on my baby's brain, not even Joan. I figured that if I didn't think about it or talk about it, it would somehow just go away.

Then the morning of my appointment arrived, and I finally had to face the possibility that the news might be bad. I decided to treat myself to a big pancake, egg and bacon breakfast while I still didn't know anything. The coffee shop I chose—one of those relics from the 1940's—was near the bus stop in midtown where I planned to meet Brian. "Can I get you something to drink?" the middle-aged coral-lipsticked waitress asked with a glance to my belly.

"I'll have a decaf. Thanks." I had a sudden craving for the taste of coffee.

The waitress shook her all-knowing head at me as if I were a child. "You really shouldn't have coffee. You know that, sweetheart. You're pregnant."

As I forced my gaping mouth closed, I realized she seemed familiar—in a sickly sweet way. Yes! She had to be Chinette's Evil Twin. They dressed and talked the same, but this one was not the Mommie-sympathizer.

Joan had told me once that a pregnant woman's mind was like *The Streets of San Francisco.* "A couple of trigger-happy detectives patrolling the neural pathways in a black-and-white with a bullhorn. It's one shakedown after another," was how she put it. "Every personal desire found loitering around the lower brain functions gets busted as a potential *Danger To The Baby.*" Knowing Joan, her brain must have been a regular policemen's ball.

But this scolding waitress was not inside my head. Apparently my inner vice squad got its tips from squealers on The Outside like her. Why was this waitress butting into my life? Hadn't she heard me? I hadn't said "triple espresso." I'd said *"decaf."* But all right. It was true. Even decaf had some miniscule percentage of caffeine in it, and caffeine was bad.

I'd tried hard to deny it, but if there turned out to be something on the baby's brain, I had to face that it was all because of me. Because I had been *using.* For months. I'd been using Coca-Cola. The real thing, *with caffeine.*

Any sense of joy while pregnant had mostly come to me through eating and drinking. Certain foods like corn, tuna sandwiches and steak tasted sensational at certain times, at least while I was eating them. But Coca-Cola was in a class by itself, helping my nausea so profoundly that the effect actually lasted for up to fifteen minutes afterwards.

The pregnancy books I'd read said caffeine intake should be limited, that is, if one chooses (*stupidly* chooses was implied) to drink caffeine at all. I'd tried to limit its use, but Coca-Cola was the only thing that could make me feel less sick for any length of time, and thus less anxious—which would make a better experience for the baby. Wouldn't it? Well? I was hanging by a thread. Besides, I never drank Diet-Coke with all those bad, bad artificial sweeteners—well, because I didn't like it. Only straight Coke with its own particular chemicals and sugar would do. And yes, the caffeine.

Coke on the brain. This baby has caffeine on the brain. My God. The damage has been done. It's too late now to even try anymore.

I was finally able to stop my obsessive thoughts and muster, "Just give me a decaf and a number seven with bacon. Thank you." Then I nearly went insane.

"But what about me?" I wanted to scream at the waitress. Do I even exist to you? Is this body my own or is it a vessel belonging to you and the United States of America? I wanted to enlist in the front lines of the Pro-Choice movement at that very moment—and would have if I'd had any energy. *How dare you?* I wanted to say to them all. *How dare you talk to me that way!*

I forced myself to enjoy that cup to the last drop. Then I set off armed with outrage to face whatever awaited me at Einstein Hospital.

Brian and I, now *Mr. and Mrs. Don't Make Us Prove How Immature We Are*, sat silently in the waiting room. Our nerves were raw by the time a very prim and demure-looking Chinese-American doctor greeted us. She beckoned us to follow her.

"Papa, be happy!" she bellowed like a truck driver, holding the sonogram up like an Oscar. "Come look at the photo!" She only seemed to want Brian. He got up and studied the sonogram with her. "See? Papa be proud! Baby has huge, huge penis!"

Brian gazed back at me. Neither of us could believe it. She stopped talking, and I had to remind her why we were there. "Excuse me, but that thing on the baby's brain? Is there a problem?"

"Oh, that was nothing," she said casually.

SO YOU'VE CREATED
A MONSTER

(or As Long As He Needs Me)

in which Joan discovers the true meaning of togetherness...

Linda had seen me in the delivery room. Seen with her own eyes that I was no longer pregnant, and yet—miraculously—not dead. Surely that was all the empirical evidence she needed to explode her childbirth-equals-death theory. Or at least puncture it.

But she still had that looming fear of losing herself in motherhood. I never tried to convince her that it was silly to think a grown woman could be overwhelmed by her baby's needs, because, in Linda's case, I wasn't so sure. If my feelings hurt, saddened and frightened her, what would she do with the onslaught of an infant's miseries?

At forty-one Linda was still more childlike than some twelve-year olds I knew. Her open-hearted spontaneity was seductive. Like a female Peter Pan. I loved it and I hated it. Three years before it had almost driven me to bestfriendicide.

Linda and I had been desperate for investors in our sci-fi film, "The Apricot Story," and it had taken me a good deal of finagling, including several goodwill visits to apricot groves and packing plants, to convince the California Apricot Advisory Board to grant us a few minutes to speak about this irresistible investment opportunity at their monthly board meeting.

To the crowd of growers packing the hall I presented my carefully prepared bars and graphs of projected grosses, and pitched a promotional package that would make the California Raisin green with envy. I finished up with assurances that the film would in no way besmirch the apricot's pristine reputation. When I stopped talking, I noticed it. The room was a morgue. Like the time I did stand-up for the Electrical Workers Union Local 435 Christmas party. With a mousey *Thank You*, I sat. And tried to hide.

Then as if we were on a see-saw Linda boinged up, writhing and cooing coquettishly about how sensuous and adorable she thought apricots were. I nearly clawed a hole in her white jacket trying to get her to shut up and sit down. I would have given her the Vulcan Neck Pinch if I'd known how. Then I heard it. The snickering. And I shut my eyes. I could picture the sea of faces grimacing at the unctuous ingénue horror. But when I looked up, they weren't grimacing. They were beaming. Apparently they found her *Gidget Goes Ga-Ga* sensuously adorable.

Okay, who wouldn't? When we didn't get the funding, I chalked it up to too much financial analysis and not enough goofy hip-swiveling. Well, Linda was a bit childish, but childishness is powerful.

Whether this would be an asset or a liability in her future motherhood I wasn't sure. Could you really fight the inevitable challenges of infancy *with* infancy?

It was the first day of my son's life. Not a time to be concerned with Linda's neuroses. As I lay in the maternity room on the thing that was supposed to be like a bed, I stared at my tiny lump of human potential and felt the pleasant intoxication of maternal zeal.

Our midwife came in, looked me over and reported in an off-hand but congratulatory tone that Graham had been "born in the caul."

Thom and I must have looked as dumb as posts, so she explained that the amniotic sac had never burst, his head was still wrapped in it as he slid into the world, and that such a birth was considered prophetic in many cultures.

It sounded to me as if he'd been trying to drag with him into the big scary world as much of the womb as he could. Had I been more aware, I might have recognized his resistance to being expelled unprotected as a message. It might have helped prepare me for what was in store.

As it was, his intensity took me by surprise. He seemed to be overly sensitive to everything: light, sound, smell, touch, separation, strangers, crowding. I learned to keep him swaddled tightly and cloak his head to prevent over-stimulation. I made a tape of vacuum cleaner noise to soothe him. He had to be held and carried no matter what I was doing—cooking, showering, vomiting. Our doctor dismissed it all with a "Relax! Why don't you let him have some fun?" Obviously some kind of Rasta-Mormon koan to free me from my prison of sensory illusion.

That's probably what the insurance company was doing as well, by rejecting every claim I submitted. According to the insurance company, not only were Graham's sensitivities my own delusions, but so was my pregnancy. They clearly stated I'd had no need for prenatal care or hospital services. Despite the help of these authorities, my sensory illusions continued.

After three months, Graham still couldn't sleep by himself, or perhaps I couldn't tolerate getting up ten times a night. So I started sleeping with him. Thom was open to the idea of a family bed. He just didn't want to be in one. So I made my nest on the couch. That meant everyone could get some rest. It also meant Graham and I were now officially attached at the hip.

At two months Graham developed colic—that malady for which no cause or cure is known today, but in a previous century was eased with an opium-laced infant cocktail. How I wished I'd been living in that time!

He would hold his little body stiff as a board, shrieking while I tried to comfort him. I bounced him until I thought my back would break. I nursed and sang and bathed, but nothing helped. In my despair, I thought of forming a colic support group, but the image of a room full of weeping parents and screeching babies seemed like a prelude to mass suicide. After two months, the colic disappeared as abruptly as it had arrived. But Graham's neediness did not.

It seemed I could never put him down without enduring the inevitable shrieking that followed any thirty-second block of "independent play." So I wore him instead.

The little blue flowered baby sack on my chest was his "pouch," and I put him on in the morning like a pair of pants. This remained his primary habitat even when his lanky two year-old legs dangled below my knees.

But I was still determined to be available to Tricia and Tim and to my mother, despite my bulky, screaming, eight-limbed awkwardness. I drove my daughter home from work once a week despite Graham's protests. I visited my son at Cal while I bounced my bundle like a caged ape woman. I cleaned my mother's house through his howling. Everyone tried to understand.

But I often felt I really couldn't be truly present to anyone but this infant. Not even to myself. It was as if I'd grown another head—the way his little noggin was always sweeping back and forth just under my chin. I was now governed by two brains. There was my nervous system and his. It was too hard to respond to both, so I decided to focus on his and squeeze mine in around the edges.

I tried one-handed typing, and even over-his-head-filming, but eventually the fingers ripping at my lips and the bodily fluids oozing over expensive equipment discouraged me.

The door was closing on my old world of writing, film-making, and comedy—of just reading the paper. Here was my new raison d'être—protecting this child. I wondered. Would I ever again climb aboard that old film projector loco-motive of my pregnancy dream? Or was I destined for a long hard ride down the interstate in that sleek and ultra compact Yugo Stepfordia?

I knew I couldn't go on without help. I understood why the friend, who'd volunteered to baby-sit for us once, politely declined further requests. But why didn't we get even one response to our ad for a sitter? Maybe people were suspicious of the steel union wages we offered.

Graham, however, wanted nothing to do with anyone besides his parents. Even drivers passing our car in the next lane were too close for comfort.

Sitting in his little car seat, his face pinched up and baring his only tooth to look as threatening as a six-month old could, he hissed out a primitive jungle warning, while his tiny out-stretched palm fended off the invaders.

Graham's world was divided into My Mommy and the Not-My-Mommies. And his Mommy was not for sharing—not even with Daddy. Graham even created a new umbilical cord between us.

It began as a comfort habit. He would jam his fingers into my mouth and hang them over my lower lip, making it impossible for me to hold a conversation. He seemed to think that damming up this leaky soul portal would prevent the escape of any Precious Mommy Essence to which he felt exclusively enti-tled. Maybe he could sense my supply was running low.

Thom had no time or energy to help. When he was home he was asleep. The one good thing was that we were both play-ing by the same rules now.

I'd felt disloyal that first year of our marriage as I watched his spirit languish in the corporate inferno, while I flitted between temp jobs so I could concentrate on writing. When my needy child changed all that, it was actually a relief. No longer would Thom come home the brain-dead cuckold to hear his wife rave about her latest tryst with the mangoat of self-actualization. Our marriage was enjoying a brief recess from inequity. We were both miserable.

It was clear there wasn't going to be any 50-50 or even 90-10 in regard to caring for Graham, and it scared me. But why did I need outside support? My mother had done it with no help from her husband. At forty she was taking care of seven of her own, a few foster children and even a foreign exchange student or two. And she'd loved (nearly) every minute of it! Maybe it was her Puritan heritage.

Because of her politics she'd never joined the Daughters of the American Revolution. But my mother was one Mayflower descendent who actually lived the Puritan Dream. Simplicity, thrift, charity, and the joy of cooking for nine gaping pie holes three times a day.

I only had one child and I wasn't sure I could do this job without some electroshock and a Sherpa. Whatever it took to be a mother—if I'd ever had it—I didn't seem have it now.

It was not only hard to keep up with Graham's neediness, it was hard to keep up with him—period. I don't think he learned to sit till he was eight. I envied mothers who could hold their children in their laps. Graham had gone straight from rolling over to running.

I'd read somewhere that the sign of Sagittarius was related to the thigh. Symbolically, I thought. Until I noticed my son's captivation. Every day after leading me on our usual two-hour chase through the neighborhood, Graham would climb onto the couch, heave himself upon the dog and bury his face in Bentley's flank.

Bentley looked like a failed genetic experiment with his huge head and tiny legs. I knew how it felt to be so top-heavy.

Trying to be the mother Graham needed I felt like I was parading around under a gigantic paper mache Mardi Gras head of The Blessed Virgin that wobbled so grotesquely on its perch, it threatened to tumble off at any moment and expose the drunken pea-brain beneath. Bentley at least maintained some dignity.

"I love his figh!" Graham would croon, rubbing his cheeks back and forth across the furry flank. As he lay sprawled in supplication to this sacred, coiled spring of motion, I figured he was either giving thanks to Mercury for the blessing of speed or praying for the secret of ballistic propulsion.

On Sundays Graham would grab a trike and line up with the other toddlers at the cyclone fence around the Kensington Unitarian Church where I was a teacher. At the eagerly awaited ka-chink of the latch he would shoot out of the gate like Sea Biscuit on Crank to disappear beyond the distant assembly hall. Frantically I would urge the others on with a barrage of praise and threats until my torpid wagon train—now a logjam of swiveling handlebars and scuffing sandals—finally inched out to the sidewalk where I could see my son on the distant horizon, shooting past the peace shrine.

And whoever told you parenting was going to be easy? The cultural taboo against maternal dissatisfaction was ever-present:

You don't know how good you've got it!

Count your blessings!

You made your bed now lie in it!

When are you going to grow up and accept responsibility?

If you can't feel something nice, don't feel anything at all!

In the Code of Martyred Motherhood, the First Commandment is *Thou Shalt Not Complain.* Of course I knew women who had it far worse than I did; I'd taken in homeless women and battered wives. I had friends whose kids had cancer. I knew full well I was the luckiest mother on the planet. For years I tried to be a properly silent good girl, never uttering a word about my selfish feelings. I'd been a mother before and I understood the Herculean workload and mind-numbing responsibility of parenthood. I just didn't get the *I can't feel my legs, back or torso anymore* part.

A back brace eased the physical agony, but what about the pain in that little bit of mind I had left? I didn't want to fall into the trap of resentment and blame. (Commandment Number Two) But I did resent. I did blame. I did fall over in a heap.

Pretty soon I was not a person who had raw nerves. I was a raw nerve with a person buried underneath. Every time I tried to comfort Graham and he would not be comforted, I felt afraid. What if I hit him? I had hit my first son once. It happened the night before I gave birth to my daughter. I was working one of my thirteen hour shifts as nanny for another toddler, raking in eight bucks a day.

The two boys were in the bath tub. There was screaming, a few polite warnings, and then swift as God's own wrath came the whap of motherly palm against cherubic flesh. The red "turkey" palm imprint on Timmy's cheek looked like a sadistic Thanksgiving art project.

Now with Graham, I seemed to be coming to a breaking point every night. It took all the emotional energy I had left over from caring for him to keep myself from quelling his neediness with brute force. What would the authorities recommend? A shopping spree? I was ready for a shooting spree.

Well then, how about the perennial wisdom of my European ancestors? Those billions and billions of mothers who'd gone before. When all else failed in those primitive villages and nomadic encampments—as it must have on a regular basis—necessity defined morality. Back then, infanticide wore a friendlier face. Everyone knew demons could steal your infant and replace it with a soulless facsimile, which then of course had to be disposed of. I could imagine the weary waves of peasantry surging up those windy plateaus to surrender their changelings. And I felt the tugging undertow of tradition.

I had always believed the difference between me and the woman serving a life term for killing her child were my opportunities for respite, mental health care and a support network. Now, as I paced the floor, locked in a duet of despair with this mocking miniature of my own helplessness I realized the only thing that could keep me off death row would be pure dumb *luck*.

My self-esteem was so low I couldn't bring myself to call a child abuse hotline for fear "They" would come haul Graham away—probably at my insistence. So I called Linda. Linda the Validator, who wouldn't judge or tell me what to do, who could pull me out of a downward spiral with a flash of her liberating offbeat perspective.

But Linda had just moved to New York and we'd been out of touch. I felt guilty calling just to use her. I never called her to say Hi or to ask how she was. I never called her at all.

I wondered why that nurturing hormone, Oxytocin, that was supposed to make females supportive and caring, wasn't helping me in that regard. I certainly had a Spanish Fly concentration racing through my veins. In fact, I was probably Oxy-toxic, but it was all channeled into my child. Not a drop left over for anyone else. I hadn't spoken to Linda in almost a year.

I swallowed my guilt; I was desperate. So reminding myself how Linda yearned to be needed, I punched in her number. When she picked up the phone, she spoke as if I hadn't neglected her for months. I babbled out my predicament and she went to work, proclaiming her confidence in me: "You are not going to hit that baby." I argued with her through my tears, but she was adamant in her reassurance.

After a long silence, I told her, "I don't feel any better."

"You don't?"

"No... I feel worse."

"Worse?"

"Yeah. I'm sorry, Linda, but I do. I'm putting a lot of energy into not choosing an option you don't think I have."

"What?"

"I feel like you think I'm not capable of murder, so there should be no problem. Hitting the baby *is* an option, and I'm working very hard not to choose it!" This was a tactic Linda had taught me, to spell out what you want, including exactly what you want other people to say to you. We used it on our husbands all the time.

"Oh," she perked up with the thrill of discovery, "you're scared you're going to do something awful!"

"Yes." I sobbed now, grateful she'd picked up her cue.

"Why don't you go out?"

Oh, God, now she's got to solve it for me. "Thom's not here." I tried to get her back on the sympathy track.

"Well, just take Graham next door."

"They don't speak English."

"So much the better. Go over there with your tear-streaked face and *mime* that your husband has just been in a car—no. No, he's had a mild heart attack in a bar. And—oh! Of course—in the arms of another woman! But, no. Not a bar. A hotel! Yeah, The Claremont Hotel! Then you say you gotta pick him up, and see? You get to go there and have yourself a nice Brandy Alexander!"

I didn't, but I was still laughing after we hung up. I bounced Graham till he fell asleep. Okay, so the Validator couldn't validate my angst. My struggle to get Linda to say what I needed to hear at least helped me to say it out loud for myself.

I made it through that night and all the rest without becoming the latest talk show Pariah. Linda was right. (Damn her!) I never hit Graham, but until he was three that nightly psychic battle raged between the Donna Reed and the Joan Crawford inside me.

As if my own tiny corner of suffering wasn't enough, there lay beyond my doorstep a world of disapproval.

While a baby on your hip may seem normal in tribal communities, here it's more common to carry one around by the handle of its infant seat. In some cultures a child doesn't cry more than six seconds before it's picked up, but in mainstream America the watchword is *independence*.

A "proper" mother weans her child away from her as early as possible. Why couldn't I make my child do *anything* without my participation? Was I lazy? Over-possessive? Maybe too insecure myself? All I needed was a dingy sideshow platform and a carnie—*See the Amazing Spineless Lady!* People looked at me like I had a social disease. And everyone had a cure.

Advice came pouring in from therapists, teachers and people behind me in lunch lines. "You can't just pick him up every time! You're creating his dependency," or "That sippy cup is depleting his will forces—you're turning him into a smoker." Wherever I went I was dished up another helping of well-intentioned shaming. Like a progressive dinner of intervention.

My inner conflicts paled next to this external rainbow of remedies. Less and less sure of my own perceptions, I became more and more intimidated by the absolute certainty of my accusers.

One friend suggested gently, "You're probably trying to make up for what you did to the other two." That certainly gave me pause. Had I concocted a whole Baron Munchausen dependency syndrome—just so I could show off my new improved caretaking skills?

If only I'd been able to invoke the redneck oracle. I could almost hear Chinette's breezy, "You'll get this pacifier away from him when you pry it out of my cold dead fingers." Her towering rat's nest probably wouldn't have done much for my credibility. But wait—maybe if I wrapped a bright turban around my head and invented some colorful costume, my child-rearing style would not be met with derision, but with that obligatory display of respect the enlightened American reserved for third world traditions. "Oh, so that's how they do it in your homeland."

But no. I was obviously just another Euro-American and there wasn't a whole village raising my child. Just me, and I was tired.

Once, when Graham was about four months old, a counselor gave me step-by-step instructions on how to let him cry for half an hour. I was supposed to begin with a five minute warm-up. So I laid him on a blanket and started counting. Louder and louder over his screams. At forty-five seconds I couldn't take any more. Ashamed, I picked him up and cried with him.

When Graham cried, I felt his pain. When he hollered, I felt his impotence. Was I supposed to ignore these feelings and leave them out of my decision-making?

Certainly in some situations I could. I wouldn't let him pull the cat's tail or stick his fingers in a light socket. Why couldn't I even occasionally override his demands for my time, attention or my body? Was I letting him tyrannize me?

I sometimes talked about Graham's needs in terms of what he "made" me do. "I have to suck his fingers or he'll scream." I realized how this sounded—as if he'd been conditioning me like one of Pavlov's dogs to submit to his will.

Have to—the victim words. They suggested I felt controlled and resentful. And, well, at times I did. Was I abnegating my authority? I had certainly heard often enough that a "responsible" mother wouldn't let her child tell her what to do. Maybe I was empathizing with him too much.

His bedroom floor was covered in wall-to-wall corn meal

because he *needed* the soothing tactile play. I replaced the lawn with several truckloads of sand, dirt and bags of old garbage because he *needed* a hill to climb. Our gravel driveway became a gigantic waterway with islands and moats because he *needed* to build dams and flood villages. Right there was enough circumstantial evidence of psychological enmeshment to get me dragged off for a good working over in some shabby back room by—well—by myself, of course.

I wished I could have confided in Linda. But it was Graham's neediness that had squeezed her out of my life. How could she support the parenting style that had estranged us?

Still, maybe there was someone who was honestly in my corner. Maybe I'd been looking for a June Cleaver to guide me through this mess, when what I really needed was a Kathleen Cleaver. As a Black Panther advocate of self-determination for developing nations—and my fantasy teen idol—wouldn't *this* Mrs. Cleaver naturally support a parent's right to self-determination in raising a developing child? In fact, if I could just merge the June and the Kathleen Within, I would have one Super Mrs. Cleaver who could probably make militant self-determination sound yummy.

But delicious as the idea was, I couldn't get around my self-doubt. That collective, all-knowing *They* seemed so inarguably right, simply because there were so many of Them and so few of me.

But why was it an aberration in this culture to nurture a child's dependency needs? Why shouldn't every crying infant be picked up in six seconds or less? The only situation where I'd seen anyone respond so fast to a cry for help was when I worked the front desk at a major corporation.

As a receptionist I'd always been reminded, "Pick up that call before the second ring!" The frantic race to answer a board lit up with calls from full-grown sales reps before their alleged six-second fuses blow is considered common courtesy. But if a mother responds to her baby in less than a minute, it's overindulgence.

My parental omnipresence continued through his preschool years. But there were plenty of parent participation schools around, and according to my stubborn Aristotelian logic—*all children loved nursery school, Graham was a child, therefore...* Well, not so fast. In three years I enrolled and withdrew him from four different schools. At every one of them Graham felt tormented by too much noise, too many children, and too little mommy. Although his attempts to bite off the appendages of any child who toddled within snapping range were gently explained away by loving teachers as "natural," I felt they might be a cry for help or a protest against becoming a face in the crowd before he knew his own face.

Eventually the facts of his life that wouldn't fit into my old theory of optimal child development began to coalesce into something new, something that made sense. It finally hit me that I'd been trying to raise him exactly as I had my first two kids, expecting the same outcome.

Even though I'd also indulged them with a family bed and years of nursing, they'd always been very independent. They had loved nursery school, visits to relatives and going off to friends' houses. But Graham was different—from his brain to his toes.

Graham needed me to be right there with him all the time. At one. At two. At three. Even at seven and eight. He needed that mantle of protection I provided. From a world that was too stimulating, too coarse, too invasive. Yes, he was that horrible word—*Dependent*. But I was that even uglier word—*OVER-PROTECTIVE*.

So what? Eventually, it became clear to me that I had failed, not because I couldn't do what every other mother seemed perfectly able to do—to train my child to sleep in his own bed, leave him in daycare, make him independent of me. My fault had been in letting outside pressures blind me to who he really was.

Maybe I'd never needed to know the "right way" to be a mother, following some culturally-imposed model. Maybe I'd just needed to learn how to be the right kind of mother for this particular child. And over the years my son had been showing me how.

Wasn't the information that surged through this visceral connection between us as valid a source of guidance as any advice from the outside? Evoking my emotions was his only way to speak to me. And deep in my heart, I think I'd always understood him.

It was the same message he'd brought to me when he'd come into this world still holding the covers over his head. "I need you to stay a part of me for a little while longer, to stand between me and the world. Give me just a few more years in the womb, and I'll be all right." And nine years later, he was.

WOMEN USED TO JUST DROP THEM IN THE FIELDS

(or Wake Me When It's Over)

in which Linda pays homage to the chemical industry...

The idea of giving birth terrified me. American women rarely die of childbirth anymore, but there was absolutely no reason why it couldn't happen to me. In fact, I was sure it would. That Joan had survived it three times was really no proof of anything. I wasn't ready to trust the glowing childbirth testimonials of a woman who loved having menstrual periods.

I'd visited her in the delivery room two years before. She had looked so tranquil as I sat there next to her. That's when I realized everything was not as it appeared to be. Something was fishy. Maybe it was that loopy smile. She was trying too hard to show how easy it was.

When I was eight and a half months' pregnant, it was highly recommended I take a tour of the hospital birthing center where I'd be delivering the baby. I was initially apprehensive about seeing where I would actually have to perform the act—aware that my view of the hospital would be tainted by my fear—but by the time the tour was over I was convinced the place was a torture chamber.

The sunny-spirited tour guide led our group of four through pasty green delivery rooms with austere shower stalls for labor pains and "homey" recovery rooms swarming with teddy bears who kept giving me diabolical looks.

We were amiably reminded of the epidurals available to ease our torment and told of the romantic candlelight dinner served to every mom and husband before discharge. Our smiling guide must have thought it unimportant to mention it would be hospital food. She reminded us once that childbirth was a beautiful thing, which, for me, was one time too many.

We passed a woman in a labor room. Only her head and feet protruded from opposite ends of a curtain as if she were a magician's assistant being sawed in half. It was hard to tear my eyes away, but I had to catch up with my group.

Down the hall I glanced through the nursery window at a just-born baby still streaked with blood, and after seeing the strained smiles from the nurses inside, I wondered—even more—what everyone was trying so hard to cover up.

That same evening, Brian and I walked up Second Avenue to one of our Lamaze classes at Beth Israel Hospital. I appreciated learning more about what to expect and how to breathe the right way. But sitting there in the midst of all those pregnant women, I had a problem imagining myself as one of them—a woman who could actually have a baby.

I had been a theatre and film actress for years, and I was good at using my imagination positively in my work. So why couldn't I simply imagine myself in this role as I had in so many others? Could I play the part of a suicidal lesbian? No problem! How about an Elizabethan psycho? Sure! But a woman giving birth? *Absolutely not!*

My ability to leap into fantasy had turned against me, pushing me instead into the darkest reaches of terror. How would I ever rise to the task of labor, to be tough enough—or even practical enough—to get on with what needed to be done?

More easily I pictured going into the depths of emotion right in the middle of it all. I saw myself screaming out in shame that I just couldn't do it, while the baby turned blue, stuck in between my legs and the world beyond until both of us finally died together in an incredible explosion of pain.

"Natural childbirth is the only way for you to go!" This decree issued from the other side of a checkered table cloth at an Italian restaurant during a girls-night-out. She was a playwright invited especially for my benefit, as we had in common our passion for writing. "Don't let them fool you!" she continued without bothering to ask what I thought about any of it.

On this frosty November evening I found myself staring into the flapping jaws of my own worst fears and self-reproach. I was just about due and her words left me speechless.

The heat didn't seem to be working in the restaurant and I shivered in my long winter coat. I was chilled to my toes, so I stuck my head down into the steam coming from my cup of minestrone to hide. But my ardent dinner companion leaned her spaniel-like face into me so close I could feel her breath. "You're not going to have a *cesarean*, are you?" she panted, as if ready to jump on me and bite my leg.

I suddenly thought of Joan, who—with all her intense opinions about so many things, including childbirth—would never speak to me that way. She had always lived in the world of paradox. She could wax rhapsodic for half an hour about natural childbirth as a woman's right, a sensuous fun ride, even an anti-imperialist act. Yet it was her closing statements that would stay with me. "But everyone's different. Only the woman giving birth knows what's right!" And even if I resented that hint of supremacy that always lingered behind Joan's diatribes, I knew that she believed in self-determination far more than she did her own ranting rhetoric. And I missed her.

Unfortunately, this woman wasn't Joan. Was she with the pregnancy patrol or what? I didn't want to argue with her, but I also wasn't able to go for the easy lie and say, "I probably won't have a cesarean." Especially since unconscious non-participatory childbirth was my absolute ideal. So I forced a polite smile and managed, "Why'd you ask?"

I sat there as she went on about why every woman should experience natural childbirth, but I held my focus on the fact that we were all going to see a play after dinner and then we wouldn't have to talk anymore.

I was too vulnerable to tell her the truth, which was the difficulty I had believing a baby could even come out of my body, at least not unless I went insane or died first. And I'd already planned on letting those intelligent and capable (I prayed) doctors do whatever they had to do if it meant the baby and I could actually live through the birth somehow.

I knew I could call Joan. She'd be there for me. In short bursts. So why wasn't I rushing to the phone? It wasn't that I really minded taking turns with the baby for her attention. Wasn't I craving her comfort? Well, no.

I was almost afraid of that infinite empathy she had, empathy that could EVEN feel compassion for me, the freak. Just hearing her voice would be the final nail in my coffin. There wasn't anyone in the world who could make me feel more miscast in the role of mother than Joan could. Joan the Righteous: going through childbirth the natural way despite the pain, doing the 24/7 with her child despite the pain. It would be like an apple talking to an orange. The more the orange explains itself the more it realizes it's not an apple, and never can be.

Maybe Joan wanted to do it all herself. But I didn't. In fact, I wanted to give *all* my responsibility away. When it came time for this birth I only hoped someone would let me hand over all my power. Please, take it all away, every bit of it! Knock me out first, of course—but then beat me, cut me, stand me on my head. Whatever it took to make it through alive was fine with me.

TRIAL BY ISOLATION

(or Across the Great Divide)

in which Joan discovers a cure for popularity...

Back when we were single aspiring actresses, Linda had asked me to represent her at an Unemployment hearing. It just took a little detective work to expose the bureaucratic blunders and she won her case. I'd done the same with her childbirth theory—using my own experience as hard evidence: I was living proof that pregnancy wasn't a fatal disease!

Before she moved away to New York, I had an opportunity to do it again. A living diorama of life with baby would dispel any lingering superstitions that motherhood was a freedom-exterminator. Boy, was she a tenderfoot!

She was coming to visit me that afternoon. Now she'd see with her own eyes that personhood and parenthood could co-exist peacefully. I picked up all the diapers, toys, blankets, baby food jars, bibs, walker, feeding trays, changing pads, baby books, laundry, half-eaten Hot Pockets, a week of spilled coffee cups, and shoved them into the bedroom. There! All evidence removed! Well—except for the filthy carpet, haunted house layers of dust, and paper diapers duct-taped to the corners of every piece of furniture. But who'd notice that? I was—oh, God—I was a mess! I'd forgotten about my disheveled hair, stained shirt and screaming baby strapped on like a bandolier.

Well, maybe I wasn't the best role model to convince her there would be an ounce of self left after the scourge of childbirth. It was obvious I didn't get out much anymore.

Graham was only a few weeks old when the reality of my isolation set in. But what had I expected? I had lived in a world of mostly single adults who were continuing their single adult working lives. Maintaining these friendships would be difficult.

But not impossible! Linda had been silently accusing me of neglecting her for a year. Now that I was post partum I would show her I could pick up our relationship right where we left off... wherever that was.

I was delighted and nervous when Linda showed up with Stewart at my door. Stewart was our poet friend—a poet in the largest, most nineteenth century connotation of the word— a one-man Aesthete Liberation Front fighting sham and mediocrity with blows of scathing social criticism. His beard spread out under his grin. Linda was jumping up and down on the porch, twirling her arms like pinwheels. I figured that meant there must have been a cease fire in one of the world's trouble spots. *(If Yitzak Rabin and Betty Boop had a child!)* but it turned out there was no news clipping in her pocket, she was just happy to see me.

Stewart went off about his grad school hassles, the latest failed romance, and a sort of folk song about how Noam Chomsky would react to the Pope's new spin on Hell. I could hear him over Graham's fussing, but it was dull and distant as if one of us were underwater. I lifted my head to nod and then submerged myself again in the wriggling bundle of needs in my lap.

As Linda jumped in with news about Israeli-Palestinian peace talks and a speeding ticket, I came up spraying an incoherent sentence fragment from my blowhole. Linda looked disappointed as she went on with less enthusiasm about moving to New York. Again I tried to listen, but my senses were tuned to another frequency.

My devoted friends struggled to maintain eye contact with me, but I just couldn't reciprocate. So they focused on the baby, as if to predict the next interruption. But that didn't help because it was only those interruptions I was paying any attention to. They were beginning to realize I couldn't respond to anything that was not relayed to me through my child.

In their frustration they must have figured that if you couldn't get *around* the baby—why not go through? Because at this point, Linda was leaning over in front of the baby's face—speaking loudly *into* him as if she were ordering something from Jack-In-The-Box. She seemed convinced his head was a communication link to my consciousness. Unfortunately, it wasn't.

I was two feet away from them and we were in separate universes. There was no dialog, just spears of monologue bouncing off my force field of motherhood. Finally, mumbling that I was not at my best, I said good-bye in the same haze that I'd said hello.

I watched Linda's face fall as she turned to leave. It was her pained look. Her *I am so let down* look. Linda's emotional states didn't just touch me, they swallowed me. And here I had broken her First Commandment.

Honor friendship held the top spot on her stone tablet. She had no parents or siblings. Naturally, friends were all-important to her. And she knew how to bring them together. Over the years many of us met and married each other because of her. She was Jackie Kennedy, Margaret Mead, and Studs Terkel all in one. In Los Angeles now, she had dozens of close friends, whose every opening night, gallery reception and cast party she was bound by honor to attend. I had not just let her down. I had offended her Dionysian value system.

But hadn't she also offended my more hearth-centered

Hestian sensibilities? Why did she refuse to understand that—on those rare occasions she took time out from her gadfly whirl to call me about her latest reason for shooting herself in the head—I could not always give her my undivided attention? I just could not empathize on demand anymore! Couldn't she see I had other obligations now? No. She didn't know the meaning of the word. Linda had a very different modus operandi. She was carrot-driven. I was stick.

It seemed everything she did, she *chose* to do. Not that she didn't make an occasional mistake—but it was her attitude I envied. It was the kind of self-actualizing stuff I'd only read about in psychology books. I never knew anyone could actually do it. And there I was—lugging around my big sack of supposed-to's, leaking a steady stream of resentment behind me. I wasn't sure if Linda was superhuman, subhuman or maybe—inhuman. But when she looked so goddamned honest and wholesome, I hated her.

Yes, she'd left that day feeling gypped. I knew she wouldn't understand until she had a child of her own. But as I closed the door behind me, I realized something else—I felt empty too. Not empty like you never had something, but empty like you lost something.

Like when you're out of work and hungry, so you take a shot. You go to Safeway and fill your cart to the brim praying they won't find out your checking account's been closed for six months, but they do and you can't tear your eyes away from that dreamy pile of steak and cheese and potato chips and Häagen-Dazs and your humiliated kids have to drag you away so you can go home—empty.

I'd expected to feel satiated after Linda's visit. Instead, it was like she'd never been there at all. Now it was becoming clear—not only was I incapable of giving much as a friend anymore—it seemed I wasn't able to receive much either, as if I were locked in a sound proof booth where no one can hear you scream.

Just as the egg seals up when the one lucky sperm fertilizes it, I seemed to be sealed up in my mother-child unity. Like being inside the pod-car of my pregnant dream, I was not in control. I couldn't even see where we were headed. It was like going over Niagara Falls in an overly-cushioned barrel.

The external world was as elusive as this baby was inseparable. Even just witnessing life "out there" was difficult. It was like watching images race by in flickering slices, the way a garden appears through the slats of a picket fence.

After awhile I let go of my old friendships. I stood alone, marooned on my deserted island of motherhood, as my old friends sailed past on pleasure boats and jet skis.

It seemed all the people I cared about could be reached only by letter (no time), phone (no quiet), or séance (Why not? Maybe I could actually make contact with my zombie husband!)

Or how about a message in a bottle? That had worked once—in a way. Maybe I was too bashful to advertise "Crazy mother seeks same," but there *was* a place that somebody might be advertising for *me*. The local parents' magazine!

I avoided the front section with its advice columns and how-to articles. In my delicate emotional state, this was like strolling through a minefield of candy-coated self-esteem bombs.

What I wanted was that little pot of gold at the back, the Calendar Liisting. This was the glimpse of sail on my unbroken horizon.

I can still remember the exhilaration. I yank it off the newsstand, rip it open and—with a surge of adrenaline—scan down the list: Day 1 through Day 31. Ah, clubs! Yes! Parents meetings!

Hope becomes compulsion and compulsion becomes desperation as I race through groups for parents of twins, Lesbian moms, Christian parents, Formerly Employed Mothers, single moms.

There are homeschooling park days, library circle days, groups for infants, for toddlers, for preschoolers. Somewhere in there is my salvation!

On I go—my heart pounding, sucking it all in. And then I crash. It's over. At least two hundred entries and not one I felt I could respond to. Was I shy? Yes. Elitist? Maybe. Mostly I was afraid.

The list sounded to me like one long nightmare of a baby shower. And to me there was almost nothing more terrifying than a baby shower.

Perhaps in ancient times this had been a ritual involving soothing mud holes, sacrificial mounds and sacred tunnels. But it seemed to me that, since then, most of the potency had been pasteurized right out of it.

There was no chanting anymore. Just cooing. The fecund mother goddess was now an aerobicized Betty Crocker, about as potent as a plastic Tiki doll.

I'd always been afraid I wouldn't be able to act ladylike long enough to fit in at these gatherings—to make small talk, to join in the never-ending chorus of "Oh how darling!" And just then I wasn't looking for a place to coo, but a place to whimper, curse and beseech a deity.

I was afraid that being with women who were not having a hard time would only amplify my own feelings of alienation. But what had I expected to find? *Miserable Misanthropic Moms?*

Didn't everybody have to start on the neutral ground of the superficial? Why couldn't I put up a pleasant façade, raise my eyebrows in wonder at the achievements of everybody else's two-year-old, and gush over the designer layette?

I probably could—for awhile. But sooner or later my dark psychic drama would erupt. *"Oh, that's so cute how she gur-*

gles! You know, you're right—it does sound like the national anthem and tell me how do you keep from jumping out a window?" It was better to remain in hiding.

Still, every month I grabbed those listings. Someday I knew I would find her. One other lonely, confused, desperate mother across the void who just wanted a safe place to say, "I can't go on."

Once upon a time I'd had friends who were mothers. Long ago in a previous life—when my first two children were little. Friends with whom I could talk about the dark side of anything. I had once belonged to a community of families—lives really touching other lives, spilling into each other. But it had taken me a few years to find them.

When my older children were babies, my world had been abysmal. Too drab to be Hell, too lurid to be anything else. I had moved out of my parents' East Bay home in 1970, a single teenage mom with a job at A&W. The only place I could afford to rent was in a sear little soul-desiccating netherworld beyond the edge of civilization, a great expanse of asphalt rumored to be the legendary birthplace of the Angry White Male.

There seemed to be two native tribes. One devoted to the accumulation of bejeweled crucifixes and automatic weapons, the other to smoking pot, souping-up Camaros and expanding domestic violence.

I realized I was a foreigner here as soon as I took my son to a local park. Timmy was playing in the sand when another two-year-old pushed him down. Not wanting to make a big deal out of it, I just helped him back up and dusted him off.

Suddenly the toddler's mother is crawling over him, black beehive flopping, two stiff side curls coming at me like meat hooks. "Make him hit back! What's wrong with you!" She smells my fear and turns away with a disgusted *you-sissy-pants-hippies-sicken-me* grunt.

My rebel boyfriend, however, blended right in whenever he dropped by—impressing the locals with amazing feats of automotive engineering, like sawing the steering wheel of my car in half. He was an adorably troubled nineteen-year old with no goals whatsoever, but he was the father of my children and I was dead set on marrying him.

I guess I was a rebel, too, pleading for matrimony in the free-love era. Yet one day my dream came true. It was a quick ceremony since he was AWOL from boot camp and on his way to military prison.

Two years later we divorced, and I escaped to the fertile oasis of Palo Alto. I thought I'd found Utopia.

It was not just the place—it was the people. And it was the times. These were the early 70's and Palo Alto was still a hot bed of experimental ideas, alternative schools, therapies, and collectives.

My children and I became part of a close network of families. It seemed there was always a consciousness raising group forming or an anti-nuclear action in the planning.

There were great conversations about politics, philosophy and social justice over tea, while children ran wild catching bees in jars. The prevailing anti-materialism camouflaged economic disparities, so my children didn't stand out as "have-nots." It was a rich abundant place to raise a family as a low-income single mom.

After my father died, I married a man just like him. That quickie marriage and divorce took me to another state—literally and metaphorically. It was in Denver I began my stand-up comedy career in a little hippie dive called Global Village, and lost my kids to the deadbeat dad whose parental irresponsibility now paled next to my own.

I came back to California with tunnel vision. Over the next ten years only two things mattered—"making it" and making ends meet until I did. Tim and Tricia came back to me as teenagers—probably because I was living in the wonderland of Santa Cruz—and put up with the meager mothering until they could move out.

Now all alone, the emptiness of my existence was becoming apparent. One night, I'd stolen back into my office building to work on a press release about the new horror film I was in. As the copier spit out reviews of *"The Dead Pit,"* I noticed I was actually salivating. Like the proverbial greedy dog I'd become so hungry for my own reflection that somewhere along the way I'd dropped the bone.

I pilfered address labels from the supply cabinet with none of my usual zeal and went home to the Berkeley basement I'd feng shuied into a sick travesty of Buddhist detachment: a borrowed computer, a box of comedy show costumes and enough chillingly perky headshots to turn Medusa to stone.

My envelope-stuffing ground to a halt as an apricot moon peeked between the curtains and rolled out a royal carpet of light across the emptiness. I realized suddenly that breaking into Hollywood no longer captivated me. I was really pretty content making the little offbeat film. And I missed having a life.

Tearing along through a white water world of single-minded adults, I felt wistful to live in the meandering flow of families again. That seemed real. Substantial.

Since my children were grown and John had died, I would have to start over from scratch. But this time I was going to make sure I did things in the right order..

Thom and I corresponded by mail for six months after I answered his personal ad. A few days after we met in person, we said, "I do," by torch light in a thatched hut at the Tropicana Hotel in Las Vegas. A year later we had Graham.

Ah, now I could enjoy all that good substantial connecting! Except that all my time was spent caring for our child and all Thom's was spent providing for him. Our moments of intimacy consisted of pushing a flatbed loader around Price Club once a month. To make matters worse, there were no other stay-at-home mothers in my neighborhood.

Okay, I'd almost accepted that my creative life was dead, but wasn't I supposed to be reborn into some delightful community of families? Where was everybody?

No wonder some mothers went back to work as soon as they could, if not out of financial need, out of sheer loneliness. I was so hungry for company I threw open my door to every stray meter reader, Jehovah's Witness and process server. The tentative bonding of coworkers in the corporate culture of which I'd once been a part began to look like a rich and wholesome social banquet.

I began taking trips with Graham, exploring parks and little villages all over the Bay Area—indulging my need for contact with the outside world and his need to explore. But on a deeper level I was stalking. It was the blood-thirsty hunt of a lone she-beast—ravenous for any carrion of community she might snatch. Like a jilted lover watches others holding hands on the beach, I surveyed my prey—partly with envy, partly with hope, mostly in slack-jawed mystification.

At one of these test sites—a small upscale park in one of the more exclusive parts of Oakland—I screwed up my courage and sat down and joined a group of well-dressed mothers sitting with their children on the edge of a large sand area. They were friendly, warm, real, and though they seemed full of high spirits, they were complaining! It was music to my ears. After a few minutes of listening intently and nodding encouragingly I realized they were talking about the mothers of the children they were hired to care for. As the only non-nanny, I slunk away to chase my son across the lawn. That's where I noticed a woman on a swing with a baby in her lap. She seemed closer to my own age, so I drifted casually by.

I put Graham on the baby swing, and she and I exchanged a few innocuous remarks before she asked if I lived in the neighborhood. "No," I answered sheepishly. "I'm from Hercules, up past Richmond in—well, not in—but in between, you know, the refineries. We were driving and you know— looking. It's so pretty here." Yep, that's me. Just another barbarian nomad sniffing around your civilization.

I stifled the urge to prostrate myself in the sandbox, but I wanted to beg: *You seem like a really neat woman. You must feel like screaming sometimes! Don't you need a friend?* Well, apparently not, because after a few more awkward minutes a nice woman came to join her. "Oh-here-you-are-what-took-you?" they chittered. Time to mosey along.

On many of our wanderings I just pushed Graham in the stroller for miles. If only I could walk long enough to make space bend or wear out seven pairs of iron shoes, maybe a magic gateway would open into The Land of Belonging.

One day after walking in Oakland for thirty or forty blocks, I found my way into a charming modest income residential area. The branches of the trees on either side of the street arched above to clasp hands in a canopy of leaves. Homely cottages crouched between three-story houses with pillared porches—all in pre-renovation condition.

Gardens emerged out of upturned back patios. A small empty lot was being cultivated between two houses. I breathed it all in and it warmed me deeply as if I were back in the Palo Alto of my past.

Though there wasn't a soul in sight, I could picture who lived here, who sat out on these old stoops till late on summer evenings, who diligently tilled the garden, whose children ran screaming and chasing between the waving rows of corn and amaranth, ripping handfuls of broccoli right off the stalk. I smiled, lost in my past life experience.

We passed a lovely alley, partly blocked by something. I turned to see what it was. A truck. Yes. A huge grip truck. The cables were spilling out of it, twisting like tentacles, some jammed into the little house set back from the road by a serpentine stone walk.

It cut off almost all of the narrow street proclaiming: WE ARE HERE FILMING. Not a Hollywood truck. There weren't six or seven of them. Just the one. Probably all the budget could handle. They would use it day and night. I knew.

This was no studio picture. No—this was somebody's little heartfelt film. Somebody's work of art. Just some naïve and ambitious guy or gal finally making that independent film after writing, sweating, borrowing, and charging the rest.

I could hear voices now from inside the house. The rise and fall of the furor that precedes the shot and the stillness that follows "Action!"

I felt sick. It was that punched-in-the-stomach shock that comes when you run into an old flame with his new girlfriend and you've got to hide because you know he'll want to introduce you two if he can just tear his mouth off her ear.

I could see now that my feet had stopped moving. One impulse urged me closer as another held me fast. My baby wriggled in the stroller telling me to "Move on!"

I moved like I was slogging through wet cement. This wasn't my world. I didn't belong here any more than I belonged in this little community I had stumbled upon. I was a stranger. Just passing through.

I trudged away, leaning into the breeze like a wind-whipped refugee, until we reached the car. Then with the baby on my hip, pacifier in my teeth, and my tears sticking my hair to my face, I caught a reflection in the side-view mirror. There with her long red hair blowing up to the sky and running make-up was Chinette.

"Honey. You don't need polite conversation. You need triage. I'm headin' up to Boomtown. Time for me to give that roulette wheel of paternity another spin." Sucking down a long raunchy drag of maternal instinct, she exhales, "Can you believe

Jimmy Bob is already three months old? Just don't need me no more. Gotta get me another bun in the oven." She snuffs the butt out in a nibbled Twinkie, and tosses the golden missile into the weeds.

"You should come with. There's guys up there waitin' in line to comfort a boozed-up broad. Bring the kid. Makes you look more pathetic. In fact, you could pass for hammered right now!"

I looked again and she was gone. I could see myself again in the mirror. But not the pathetic social misfit. No, it was a spunky middle-aged loner determined to survive in an alien world! *BOGEYMOM—THE QUEST FOR CLAN.*

Suddenly I realized this failure to consummate community wasn't the tragic ending to my melodrama. It was just a single episode. A turning point, from which the main character was supposed to learn a little something about alienation, desperation—and what happens when you push a stroller too far. I smiled in relief. This was just the plot twist leading up to the nude beach scene between Spartacus and my eighth grade teacher, Mrs. Harris.

When I got home, I opened my dusty laptop, sitting as far back from it as I could so that my second tiny pair of hands couldn't reach the keyboard. Waiting for the computer to warm up, I was still disturbed about my inability to make friends. But I reminded myself that there had always been those dark times when I was new in town, with no one to confide in, no one to provide comfort or perspective.

I was grateful Linda hadn't let me disappear from her life. Even if she was 3,000 miles away, I felt desperate for her to read my words. Maybe I didn't need a new social life as much as I needed to be known and understood by one true friend. And maybe she wouldn't be able to understand. But unless I told her, she'd never have a chance to try.

The computer screen glowed harshly in the twilight-filled

room. I restrained Graham with one hand and banged keys with the other, my tears dribbling into his curls. Too much self-pity? I don't think so. Not with the Durable-But-Disposable Chinette Sleazak playing me.

JACK BE NIMBLE, JACK BE QUICK

(or How to Sabotage Your Own Birthing Experience)

in which Linda takes the Devil's road to maternity...

If you told Joan that you were Fidel Castro, she would probably just nod her head and say, "That sounds hard." She was very understanding about emotional difficulties. Maybe because she'd had so many of her own.

Joan had never tried to convince me I would not die in childbirth, and I'd never suggested she lengthen the leash Graham had her on. This respect for the other's integrity was the cornerstone of our friendship. Our *Prime Directive*. A pact of non-interference we took a lot more seriously than Captain Kirk ever did. Of course, there were those rare occasions when I couldn't disguise the shock or disgust in my voice—and that's when the fur would fly.

Joan's interpretation of the pact was a little broader than mine. For her the goal was nothing short of absolute unconditional acceptance—attainable, in my opinion, only if you were a Bhodi Satva named Lenny Bruce. I had to admire Joan's determination, though, to single-handedly keep the Human Potential Movement alive.

Listening was her métier. When she wasn't feeling defensive, paranoid, pretentious or depressed, she had a special gift to offer. It was an empathic sensitivity that made Carl Rogers look controlling. Because she wasn't busy analyzing or solving my problem for me, I could work my way closer to the real core of the problem. Even though I tried to do the same for her, I knew she was getting the short end of the stick. Still, I was a good friend in other ways. I knew a lot more about having fun!

When we lived in the Bay Area, there were a couple of years Joan didn't have a car. So when she was a little depressed I used to take her on scenic jaunts to Larkspur or Calistoga.

Usually because of my brilliant planning, everything went beautifully. But sometimes we'd wander through a patch of seemingly innocuous terrain or enter some generic building that would trigger her phobic reaction to bridges, crowds, or wallpaper scenes of Grecian urns. That would put a damper on the day.

In a way I envied Joan's panoply of neuroses. She had an arsenal of devices to shut herself off from reality. I had exactly one coping strategy. Avoidance.

When a situation terrifies me, I pretend it isn't happening. Consequently, my way of coping with the horror that I was actually about to have a baby was to ignore it.

Even though I was meticulous in organizing my to-do-list, childbirth was not on it. I put very little effort into making sure I'd get to the hospital smoothly when the time came. Maybe it was because I was so used to all the difficulties I'd had getting to my pre-natal appointments.

I kept my Kaiser health insurance from California when I moved to New York, and became pregnant knowing that the nearest Kaiser clinic was far outside the city itself. I didn't have a car, but then who has a car in New York City? So first I had to take a subway to Grand Central Station, then a forty-minute train ride, then a twenty-minute shuttle bus ride from the train station, until I finally arrived at the clinic in White Plains.

I got used to the commute and enjoyed looking out the windows of the Metro-North train as we passed through Westchester County towns like Tuckahoe and Scarsdale, watching the trees along the way transform over the nine months from leafless to blossomed, from green to autumn colors. It was some comfort to see that Nature seemed to know what she was doing, even if I didn't. Of course, Brian and I knew we'd need to find a faster, more private mode of transportation for the day when I'd have to be admitted to White Plains Hospital.

Brian checked out a cheap rent-a-car place near us on Thirteenth Street with cars available at all hours. I read the "what to take to the hospital" chapter in my pregnancy book, but the way the words jumped out at me! It was the first time I'd realized I would be going there—not to drink tea and chit-chat with the nursing staff—but *to have a baby!* Well, it scared me enough to never want to open another book again.

So that was about as much thought as I could bear giving it.

I was a week overdue, but gave it no attention and went to work for a few days more until the morning before I went into labor. It was my way of pretending nothing out of the ordinary was about to happen.

"I have to finish typing this report, and I'd better call Mr. So-and-So, and I'm going to have a baby, and there's a staff meeting at two p.m.—" Showing up at the office every day was definitely not to prove how career-oriented or tough I was. In my case, work was an escape from reality. My life was not about to drastically change. I was not about to be scared to death.

They told me at prenatal classes I would know it was time to go to the hospital if my water broke or if I had contractions five minutes apart for half an hour. "Keep track of your contractions. Write them down." Quite simple—until the time came.

I stayed home from work because of pains during the night. Then all morning and afternoon my contractions went back and forth—ten minutes apart, five minutes apart, five minutes apart, ten minutes apart, five minutes apart, five minutes apart, ten minutes apart—until I'd filled a whole notebook and was ready to scream. My phone call to a midwife at Kaiser for help did anything but relieve my anxiety.

She told me to look for "contractions five minutes apart for half an hour." Gee. Thanks. *But hadn't I already been doing that?*

No one had ever mentioned this short-long scenario to me, and no one I spoke to that afternoon over the phone had anything to tell me besides that annoyingly useless refrain "a half-hour of contractions five minutes apart."

But the short-long intervals never changed, and the pain from the contractions was getting worse on a straight upward continuum, so I told Brian we'd better get the hell up to the Kaiser clinic in White Plains. They could assure us I was ready to be admitted and end my confusion once and for all.

We set out on a dark gray Tuesday evening at the height of evening rush hour. "I can't remember the last time I've driven a car," Brian said nervously. "Maybe ten years."

I almost fell on the floor. "Ten years?" I sputtered with anger, my face turning hot. "Shouldn't we have talked about this? Shouldn't you have practiced or something?" My lips shook uncontrollably. Brian didn't answer. "Owwww!" I cried, as a contraction ripped through me.

The traffic on the expressway was moving at no more than twenty-five miles an hour—stopping and starting, stopping and starting. My hastily scribbled directions were not only confusing, but also nearly illegible, and if that weren't enough, it began to rain.

After some poking, pushing and fumbling around the steering column, Brian finally figured out how to turn on the windshield wipers. A few seconds after this accomplishment the rain stopped for good and then he couldn't shut them off.

I tried to help him in between contractions, but with no success. With each deafening scrape of rubber against the glass, the pain in my belly—now expanded to my head—kept getting worse.

"Don't do this to me!" I wailed. "Can't you turn them off? It's making me insane!"

"So now it's my fault. Great." Brian sat there stiffly with his jaw clenched, looking like a stick of dynamite about to detonate.

"Well, why did you have to pick such a cheap car place?" I whined, my disappointment in him soaring to a new zenith.

"I didn't notice you looking for somewhere better!" he shouted back.

"God, why are you yelling at me?"

Heightening my despair was the growing awareness that neither of us had ever been to White Plains in a car. There had been no trial run. My coping mechanism of playing everything down had begun to backfire.

I screamed at Brian to get off the expressway so we could get calm and figure out my bad directions together. Maybe we could even find a way to shut off the windshield wipers. He yelled that if we got off the expressway we would never be able to find our way back. I forced him to get off with my oftused: "I'll kill myself if we don't! I mean it!"

He gave me his "That does it" look and pulled the car into a gas station parking lot, where we fumed silently and then went over the directions to the clinic. We even managed to shut off the windshield wipers.

For a brief moment we were friends again until Brian found out, just when we were ready to go, that he could not release the emergency brake. Nothing he tried would work. I waited for my contraction to end before yelling at him. "This parking lot's completely flat! What kind of idiot would put on the emergency brake?"

Brian looked at me with absolute, unreserved loathing. "You make me sick."

I nearly bit him. "You'll never know how REPULSIVE it is going through this with YOU!" I screamed.

"I know what it's like being in Hell," he sneered, saliva oozing from his teeth.

"OWWWWW!!! God, do you get some kind of sick pleasure making my pain worse? Do you like it? Well?"

"GODDAMN IT! SHUT THE FUCK UP!" At that point Brian nearly tore the emergency brake out of the car and somehow we were on our way. I slumped sullenly as I remembered the bizarre behavior of some of the addicts I'd known back when I'd been a rehab counselor. Brian and I had just outdone them all.

All I kept thinking, to make myself feel even more terrible, was: This is not the way it's supposed to be. This is not the way it's supposed to be. Like a mantra, which gradually evolved into: *I can get a divorce right after. I can get a divorce right after.*

We didn't speak to each other even once until we reached White Plains. We had to speak then because after we got off the expressway, we couldn't find the hospital.

This was the same place I'd been visiting regularly for nine months. White Plains is not a big place. But the directions I had were a real mess, and it had started to rain again, making it hard to see.

Without the luxury of a cell phone, we would have had to stop at a phone booth to call for better directions—something I felt we had no time to do, especially when I was so sure we were extremely close. But we kept ending up at the same distinct landmark over and over—a stop sign with eight sides, red, and with white letters—that always led me to believe we were only a couple of blocks away.

I began to wonder if the clinic had actually vanished into the gray mist enveloping us. Finally I pointed to a phone booth. We parked and Brian asked me to get out and call for directions.

"Are you kidding?" I screamed. "How gallant! So when should I call? Before my next burst of pain or after?"

Here I was—married to the stupidest man on earth, lost in a raging storm in a crappy car on the way to doing something I was sure would kill me anyway! Maybe I'd be better off locking myself in the peace and quiet of the phone booth until the baby came!

Actually, I understood that asking for directions and talking on the phone were two experiences that filled Brian with great anxiety. He really wasn't a thoughtless person. But this was also not the time for me to be sympathetic to his problems.

I staggered out of the car into the rain, wedged my way into the grungy booth and sank down on the floor. I couldn't stop sobbing. "What fools we are!" I cried out to the universe with my arms raised, strands of hair tangled in my mouth. "Such fools!" I don't know how I was finally able to call and take down the directions, but when I did, I found out we were only a block away.

Inside the car, after yelling at each other some more, we finally got to the clinic, where the doctor told me I had barely started to dilate and wasn't close to being ready for admission to the hospital.

"NO!" I cried. "We can't go back to the city! You have to get them to admit me! You have to!"

"You have to," Brian echoed. "WE CANNOT GO BACK TO THE CITY." We finally had a common enemy, and from that moment on the two of us were deeply united.

When the doctor left to take a phone call, Brian and I forgave each other our ugly displays. I had wanted him to be more like a father to me. I knew he'd have liked a father of his own there to help him out.

He confessed that he hadn't gone to the phone booth himself because he was terrified of what might happen if, even for a second, he took his hands off the steering wheel. He had to be in control and ready to go. I told him I understood. These were extreme circumstances.

"Why not get a motel room?" the doctor asked upon returning. "Or there's the Galleria mall near the hospital and you could walk around. Go shopping to take your mind off it. After a while you might be ready."

There I was having contractions in his examining room, and this doctor had actually suggested I go shopping, which—even on my best days—is my least favorite activity in the world.

Or I could go to a motel. I'd always thought of a motel as a place you go to have sex, which is what had gotten me into this situation in the first place. I also considered it to be unthinkably bleak and depressing to go through labor pains in some strange motel room. Brian and I left and drove straight to the hospital.

We hurried inside where we immediately begged, cried, pleaded and practically screamed for them to admit me early. The two admission clerks looked at us, then at each other. The older woman fumbled with her clipboard. She made a phone call, asked about available rooms, then hung up and turned silent.

The phone buzzed back, and the young man working with her answered it. His conversation had nothing to do with us. The woman made another phone call to a doctor or a nurse or somebody. Brian said later that those five minutes felt like fifteen hours as the hospital clerks made one final call, looked at each other pensively, glanced back at us, and finally pronounced their verdict.

"All right," the young man said. "We'll let you in."

Afterwards came a long night of contractions with morphine induced half-sleep, then a long morning and afternoon of more pain. After what seemed like weeks of agony, the midwife told me, "You're not dilating much," a damning proclamation that has, I'm sure, unhinged millions of women in agony throughout the centuries.

I felt like giving up, until at last the cavalry showed up with potossin and an epidural chaser, and everything seemed a bit better.

Brian asked the doctor if he had time to return the rental car back to Manhattan before my pushing began so we wouldn't have to pay for an extra day.

Although it seemed outrageous, I wasn't upset. As long as he was back before the pushing part, I really didn't care. We'd planned for my mother-in-law to bring us home, and more often than not Brian had seemed in the way.

"I'd have time to take the train back up here from the city and a taxi to the hospital?" he continued, just to make sure the doctor understood how long he would be.

"You'll have plenty of time," the doctor answered. "Time to spare." Hearing those words as I lay there moaning and groaning was not reassuring. However, in giving birth, there is no giving up. I learned that going through the actual experience was far preferable to going through the horror of imagining it. I actually managed to get through each part of the experience, and kept on getting through it just like everyone else did, even when I thought I couldn't.

By the time I was ready to push, Brian was back, and Jack was out in twenty short minutes.

I was incredibly fortunate. Brian and I looked at each other and smiled. We were still together.

Jack was laid on my chest, and I could tell right away we had named him right. *Have ya met my buddy, Jack? Oh yeah, Jack. Great guy!*

Jack. I thanked him for shooting out so fast there at the end, for being such a considerate kid. I felt truly at peace for the first time in nine months.

Love was not what I was feeling, at least not yet. I just really liked him. A lot. He was so easygoing and good-natured. So tolerant of his parents, as if he'd known what he was getting into and wanted to reassure me that anyone still breathing could take care of a baby like him.

"Good to be here," he kept saying with his eyes. "So, Mom, what's up?"

I USED TO BE SOMEBODY

(or Don't Call Me Mother)

in which Joan has an identity crisis...

Alienation loves company, and finally it happened. At last. Linda was a mother, too. Our lives were back in synch. Those unspoken but insidious judgments of hers would cease.

Certainly any day now I'd get a phone call and she'd say it. Those words I'd been waiting to hear: "I get it now." Maybe with a subtext of awe-struck admiration for all I'd been suffering through. "Oh, Joan, I never knew," or "Oh, Joan what a stupid, stupid woman I've been. Can you ever forgive me?" Even a hang-dog "You told me so!" would do just fine. At last she'd forgive me for having a child who was needier than she was.

But she didn't call. Well, understandable. A new baby and all. (Understandable to me anyway!) So I called her. "How's it going?" I baited.

"Oh.... God."

Her moaning was like music. I felt as if two great hands were sweeping us up into one pleading pair lifted to the heavens for mercy.

"Not what you expected?" I tried not to gloat.

"Not! At! All!"

"Yeah," I spewed sympathy for my new compatriot.

"HE—" she could barely get the words out.

Yes

"—IS—"

Yes, yes, I silently urged, *Go ahead and say it!*

"—SO EASY!"

I think I stopped breathing. The only sound I could make was to choke back my bile. I hoped she took that as irrepressible enthusiasm.

"I don't have to do anything! I just tuck him under my arm like a football and he goes anywhere. This is so great! I had no idea."

I giggled like an imbecile thinking about her prancing down the field with her football while I crawled on my belly beneath a medicine ball filled with concrete. She went on to tell me about how her friends were getting in line to babysit. I felt sick. Nobody wanted to get close enough to throw mine a slab of raw meat! I told her I had to go. My own life of Riley was waiting for me.

God. I felt sick. How could she ever understand now? In fact, her blithe and bonny child was probably proof to her that I'd been deliberately neglecting our friendship.

But I realized it takes more than an easy baby to bypass all the major and minor nightmares of motherhood. Babies and motherhood are indeed distinctly different entities. Yet, as time passed it looked like her motherhood and mine were going to become as distinctly different as our babies were.

My experience as the deeply entrenched stay-at-home mom and hers as the working/struggling writer mom only pulled us farther and farther apart until we seemed to live on either side of a Great Wall of Silence. Motherhood's dark side had many twisting corridors, but I had no idea it would actually take us years to find each other in that labyrinth.

Gradually I came to understand that what seemed to cause Linda the most trouble was not the baby—Jack's phantom existence never seemed to create so much as a speed bump in her fast lane social life. Her real problem with motherhood crawled out of a hole in her own psyche. It was that lifelong and all-permeating sense of being "too" different—wanting, fearing, feeling different things than "normal" people.

But instead of trying to change, she stuck firmly to her own abnormal Weltanschauung. That's what had always amazed me about her—how she could feel so hopeless and so determined at the same time. It was inspiring, like singing folksongs on a sinking raft. Her perseverance in writing was similar to her childbirth experience. Even though she felt doomed to failure, there was nothing to do but go on.

When I first met Linda, it was partly her ability to carry this duality of futility and necessity that attracted me. It seemed so starkly existential and yet mystically transcendent. Even though she had great difficulty imagining success, she kept working away at her novel year in and year out. This paradox didn't make her life easier, just livable.

For me, it was just the opposite. Over-confidence kept me going. Maybe it had merely been a rationalization for diverting precious hours away from earning income for my children. But the tantalizing mirage of a prosperous future helped me survive the day job drudgery. Self-indulgence had masqueraded freely as "investment in my future lucrative career" until that day it came face to face with Martyrdom Incarnate—my mother.

At thirty-eight, when my first two kids were just crossing the threshold of adulthood, I was between apartments as well as gigs, and looking for a job in the Bay Area. Naturally, as the perennial family freeloader, I moved back into Mom's house. After a couple of weeks of steady temping, I found myself without an assignment one morning. I was spreading my screenplay out lovingly scene by scene across the little bed, grateful and greedy for some time to work on it during daylight hours, when suddenly my mother appeared in the doorway wondering why I was still home and still unemployed.

As she mustered every ounce of that Puritan ancestral memory to suppress her disgust, I followed her shocked gaze to the patchwork of pages, and stared with her until the obscenity of it was obvious to me too. I blushed.

There was my sainted great grandmother's quilt, slathered with the effluence of my self-gratification—a violated receptacle for my writing orgy. My little offbeat screenplay felt like a dirty movie now. It was as if I were ten years old and my mother had caught me doing the unmentionable. Stiffly she retreated with a curt, "Have you checked the want ads?"

Even though it had taken all of ten minutes to rise above my embarrassment and get back to work on the film, the naughty connection between carnal pleasure and wanton creativity began to gnaw away at the back of my brain. Back in those cramped musty archives the old tapes from my teenage years played on: *Pleasure is selfish and your selfishness makes others suffer.* The haunting love theme of my life.

Luckily, the certainty of impending success shouted down all inner conflict. Although what I called *impending,* others called *illusory,* I was as intrepid as Linda was insecure. It was that penchant for rising above reality that kept me writing with one hand, while throwing caution to the wind with the other. Even with her own burden of self-doubt, Linda was the one person who would never ask me to weigh my creativity against profit, market analyses or how much I spent making props out of foam core board, turkey basters and old shower heads.

We had both grown up tap dancing and acting in the thin, but enticing shaft of limelight that flickers through the women's clubs, community theatres and recital halls. As adults, I suppose we just couldn't stop. Neither my gut-cleansing stage fright nor her unrelenting despair reined in our ambitions. I don't know if it was heredity or environment that kept us going.

Did we get just enough attention to encourage us along? Had we been deluded by our own self-serving notion of what really constituted failure? Or maybe this need to express ourselves was just innately irrepressible.

Whatever the reason, we couldn't give up our dreams. Like the other soon-to-be-famous wannabes, kooks and neo-Bohemians in the city, we diversified to get that role—any role. My publicity declared me a comedian, actress, filmmaker, writer, and professional laugher. I had multiple identities. I would never have guessed that in just a few years I would have none.

I was headed straight for a fork in my road—Hollywood or Home-making. I found myself on the road more traveled.

It seems that ever since the demise of matrifocal culture, the idolatry of Motherhood has been teetering on a shaky patriarchal pedestal, only to be knocked down, smashed and reconstituted into a more palatable form by each succeeding value system. And women like me have been adjusting, maladjusting—or just cross-dressing—down through the ages.

Up till Graham's birth I'd had an identity. I was an aspiring writer who happened to be a mother. During the 70's and 80's, post-liberation ideology had set Career up on that pedestal next to Motherhood. I fit right in as a single mother, wedging whole minutes of quality time with my kids between word-processing, comedy gigs and serial eviction. Somehow, my two amazing children made it to adulthood.

But then came the 90's—that decade of corporate deification even the apocalyptic sword of the new millennium could not smite. Motherhood was no longer *on* the pedestal. It *was* the pedestal. Supporting all the really important stuff. That was the decade I had Graham.

With a good solid husband, I was figuring on churning out dozens of screenplays between margaritas on the patio, while my infant son frolicked in the heather. Graham figured differently. By the time we moved from the Bay Area to a small Sierra Nevada community, I hadn't written in three years. A young but vigorous cultural revolution—about forty pounds of creeping, squalling proletariat—had declared Maternal Martial Law over my petty bourgeois urges.

I was the mother of a high need child. Period. End of Bio. Like the mountains around me that had once cradled the sea, my identity was going through a torpid tectonic upheaval.

But I'd be danged if I couldn't adjust. I shed the skin of my creative past and donned the long skirt and clodhopper shoes of the mountain matriarch. Maybe that's why people in Dutch Flat were so friendly. Like pioneers, they'd all left the past behind.

Well, I seemed to be a member of the club. Even though I was a newcomer, everyone waved and nodded to me—a pleasant small town convention of assumed familiarity. There wasn't much privacy in a community of two hundred. Your name might be a mystery, but your life was an open book.

My reputation spread quickly—not for my work in the theatre, but as "the one who lets her kid pee in the yard." It disturbed me. Not because it disparaged my permissiveness. It was the implication that I was *just* a mother. Even "that *has-been* who lets her kid pee outside," would have sounded better to me.

My mortification surprised me. Why was I so uncomfortable about being *just a mother?* It was not as if there was anything I was doing *besides* parenting. It certainly wasn't that I considered mothering a trivial endeavor. In fact, most of the time it seemed to be such a daunting commission I felt inadequate.

One day at a library story hour, I struck up a conversation with a friendly young mother. A conversation that didn't include the words Brazelton, Bradley, or Barney.

I sensed I'd met a kindred spirit who might understand the loss of identity that I'd been experiencing. At some completely inappropriate moment in the conversation—most of my social skills having atrophied since Graham's birth—I blurted out something stupid about being a filmmaker.

"I mean, I used to be," I clarified, flushing. "Not now." How pitiful to be grasping at the past for some validation of my worth.

Her eyes softened with recognition and acceptance. "I used to model," she said with a wide smile. "I used to *be* somebody."

Motherhood might be revered in poetry, but outside the subcultures that support the one-earner nuclear family, staying at home with one's child is often considered a waste of a woman's talents and education. And although the Women's Movement declares every mother a working mother, I'm not so sure. Because, if there's no pay, no Social Security and no time off, how can it really be bonafide labor? Unless. *Unless* you're taking care of someone *else's* child.

If you're a nanny, a teacher, a foster parent—well, that's worth a paycheck. Even the federal government will pay a poor working mother's childcare provider to watch her three-year-old, but it won't pay that *mother* to do the same job at home.

Evidently, caring for one's *own* child is not real *work*. Even the legitimate profession of caring for other people's children has always been low wage labor, historically the kind a "lady" left to her servants. And lucky she did because they were probably a good deal more knowledgeable about it than she was.

Caretaking—whether with children, the sick or the old— seems to be antithetical, maybe even heretical to the paradigm of individualism. India's lowest caste cares for the dead. America's cares for the dependent.

But if child-rearing were indeed a job *anyone* could do, C.P.S. wouldn't stand for Child Protective Services, it would stand for *Creative Parenting Society*. The most common trigger for abuse is a parent's unrealistic expectations of a child.

We aren't born with instincts for understanding child development—we have to learn. And as the child grows and changes, so also does what we need to know. In what other occupation are the raw materials, tools, product, producer and environment all constantly evolving? The learning curve can be downright Sisyphean.

Perhaps because there's no Ph.D. in mothering, it's still considered unskilled labor. We accept that becoming a professional dog trainer demands extensive education. But how to raise a human being is supposed to come naturally.

Even though I held fast to my own minority viewpoint that mothering was an important and challenging job, I felt nervous about telling other women, "I'm a stay-at-home mother. That's what I do." Why not just say, "I'm a lazy slob—that's my bag."

Before the 60's, it was different. Mothering was all a woman was "supposed to do." Now, there seemed to be a great deal of ambivalence toward it. Maybe my choice aroused a secret dread: the prospect of returning to the Dark Ages of enforced biological destiny.

I did my best to avoid the subject. Even with Linda. My parenting trials seemed petty in comparison to the anguish of her daily grind. If she asked me anything about Graham, I deferred to what seemed the far more important concerns of her WORK and her WRITING with a swift, "Nothing new." It never occurred to me that parenting was WORK, too, and perhaps just as worthy of discussion.

With strangers I kept my occupation secret. If asked point blank, I'd mutter something incomprehensible about an "off-site," "being post-proactive" or "experiments in my basement I'd rather not discuss."

Occasionally, however, my true identity *was* revealed, and the "M" word evoked some intense reactions.

"Don't you have a job?"

How could I argue with that? Mothering wasn't really so much a job as a sanity hearing.

At least the incredulous, "What do you *do* all day long?" allowed me to confess my sins before I was burned at the stake. Actually, it might have been more to the point to offer the shorter list of what I *didn't* do all day long, like sit down or eat off a plate.

The most common response to my admission of stay-at-home motherhood was also the most disturbing—a tortured mixture of grief, anger, and helplessness. "I can't stay home with my kids! I have to *work!*" I knew the unspoken *"Go to Hell, you indolent slattern"* was the flip side of frustration, and perhaps, envy. But it was painful to recognize that so many women desperately wanted and could not have what a fluke of fortune had given me—the privilege of being a stay-at-home mom.

I felt guilty for having a well-employed husband, yet I'd always advocated for social changes that could make my "privilege" an option for all families—with or without husbands. So why was I the enemy? Couldn't we resurrect a little solidarity, chain ourselves to some federal fences and leaflet our way to liberation? Where had all the sisterhood gone?

Apparently it wasn't tactful to go around telling people you were a mother. It was better if you could tuck it in around a less inflammatory occupation. *I'm a consultant for BFD Systems and I gottacouplakids.* Declare your "real" job and mumble the rest.

Even if you could muster the courage to put mothering first, you still had to have that *"and."* Just being a mother was too controversial.

I felt small and silent in my new role. But why was I buying into this jobism? Letting myself be defined by how I earned money? Why did I need validation from the *outside at all*? Couldn't I get it from the *inside*? I wasn't completely spiritually bankrupt, was I?

Maybe not completely, but I missed the easy reinforcement

that working on the "outside" brought: paychecks, vacations, raises, bonuses, free pastries. Even the onerous deadlines offered at least an illusion of closure, achievement, progress, and a chance to exhale between projects. With parenthood there is no exhaling.

Gone were the awards, applause and the little cult fan clubs. Nobody stopped me on the street now to tell me how they loved my "Medea-like soliloquy in that raw and pithy scene where the toddler drags a hose in and floods the bedroom." Yet, why did my culture reward me more for making a movie than for making a person?

Looking back, I wasn't sure how much I really liked the self-involved publicity-hog who used to get all that attention. But it was tough getting used to being a nobody.

When Graham was about seven, I spent a night in the hospital getting an emergency blood transfusion for anemia that would soon be cured by a hysterectomy. Afterwards, there were the usual forms to fill out. I scribbled away down the page until I came to the question, "What is your occupation?" It stopped me dead. Yes—*who was I?* That was the question. How that smug little blank taunted me.

I might be able to rally with "Define *occupation*" or "Answer hazy, try again later." If it meant occupation in the military conquest sense, I could just put "Graham." But how could they expect an accurate answer *now*—when more than half the blood coursing through my very veins belonged to somebody else. Yet surely there was some acceptable euphemism for what I did. How about *Bio-developmental Social Engineering Systems Analyst III?* Or maybe not. Well, what then? I panicked.

This was more than just an intake form, I realized, giving in to the intoxicating thrill of full-blown paranoia. Like the Gestapo, like the INS, like the Rainbow Girls, this was a demand for proof of legitimacy. I found myself bobbing and weaving in a deathmatch with the stigma of stay-at-home moth-erhood. A Clash of the Titans on the dark side of my identity crisis.

At last, panting and sweating, something jerked my hand across the paper as if it were a Ouija board. "Teacher-writer" was what slowly appeared in the overly-cautious hand of a sec-ond grader, as if the words themselves might jump off the page to escape complicity in my deception. But, come on—I'd been a nursery school teacher, was currently homeschooling my son—and didn't I have dozens of scripts and videos packed away in boxes? (At least the ones that hadn't been taped over with *Mr. Rogers' Neighborhood.*) There seemed to be plenty of justification for my response, but Frau Doktor challenged me.

"What is your occupation?"

Oh, dear, here it comes: *Are you now or have you ever been...?*

She pushed through my hesitation, "Would you say you were a homemaker? Unemployed?"

I began to squirm. How could I be unemployed? I was too exhausted. That meant I had to be a—*Oh, God, no!*

I smiled benignly as I pondered the ceiling grate—how I might kick it in with both Birkenstocks and haul myself up through the air duct. Then I cracked.

"Homemaker," I sniveled, ready to be marched off to Re-Liberation Camp.

Okay, so I wasn't *Somebody.* I was Somebody's mother.

But actually—a Pretty Wonderful Somebody's mother. Yes, he was pretty wonderful. I found myself settling into a quiet humility, until she referred to my film and theatre work as "hobbies," and umbrage became fury.

But why? Because some authority figure with a clipboard thought I was a phony? Maybe I was. I wasn't primarily a film-maker or writer or actress. I *was now and had been* a mother most of my life. It wasn't all of me, but it would undoubtedly be the most significant role I would ever play.

So maybe it was time for me to come out of the closet and speak those unspeakable words. "I'm a mother." No "*and.*" No excuses. No apology. Just bringing to the surface what I had always felt deep down, beneath the shifting crustal plates of personae. That motherhood was valuable and enjoyable. And that being Somebody's mother was a perfectly respectable Somebody to be.

EASY BABY,
DIFFICULT MOTHER

(or A Practical Mom's Guide
to Ignoring Advice)

in which Linda questions her insanity...

All through my pregnancy I was terrified that a baby would swallow up my life and personality. I had seen the once spirited Joan whittled down by motherhood to a bedraggled scrap of comatose electrolytes. Maybe I was more like Joan than I really wanted to be. Yet, at the same time, I worried I wasn't *enough* like her—the way she sacrificed everything for her child.

Could I really put all my baby's needs ahead of my own? Would I be able to suppress, postpone and trivialize my own creative life out of existence? Well, nobody could forever. Even full time mothers got a break when the kids started school. But apparently Joan had given up any hope of relief. Our most recent phone call ended on her cheery note of resignation, "Only sixteen more years and we can make another movie!" I pretended to laugh, and hung up, horrified. She was serious.

I was part of that heap she was bulldozing to make way for The New Development. I could see myself being scooped up by those massive blades along with camera equipment, computers, books and other distractions she wouldn't be needing anymore, while thousands of workers erected the sacred *Tower of Baby.*

Using Joan as a model for parenthood was like using a fun house mirror—you look bad no matter what you do. But even if I could be as self-denying a mom as Joan, what if, after scrapping my personal life, I discovered I was too lame-brained to figure out how to meet the endless, ever-changing needs of an infant? Especially one like Joan had!

I tried to remember what I'd learned from a more conventional (if sometimes patronizing) source: the baby care books.

Their golden rule was "Don't worry." Right alongside their pages of advice and lists of regulations was their strong assurance that if I trusted my instincts, everything would fall into place.

But who said I had any? Would I know them if I had them? What were motherly instincts, anyway? Then Jack arrived and one look at him told me I could stop worrying about maternal instincts. Apparently I wouldn't be needing any.

Holding him in my arms in those first moments, I immediately sensed his lighthearted, easygoing nature—it seemed absolutely impossible for a baby like him to ever "swallow up" my life. As I lay there in amazement, watching him figure out how to latch on and breastfeed in less than five seconds, I really had to wonder. Who was taking care of whom? I may not have had any instincts, but he sure did—as was evident in his deep understanding of the kind of mother he'd been given.

Had it been the luck of the draw? Or do children choose their parents as some would say? Was it even in the realm of human possibility that Jack would choose me, Ms. *I-Really-Want-A-Baby-But-Not-Really* for a mother? It would take such profound bravery on his part! At the time it felt far more as if I'd chosen him.

Without much thought I decided I would try to reinforce Jack's seemingly tolerant, nonchalant attitude toward whatever I did and didn't do. It helped me greatly for him to be that way. But even more, it helped me to *think* of him as being that way. Maybe you couldn't really reinforce someone's innate nature, but you certainly could reinforce your perception of it.

There was a wedding Brian and I very much wanted to attend in Baltimore. Sure, we adored the bride and groom—but the invitation included a scenic train ride and free hotel suite. How could we pass that up?

My idea was that Jack could stay on Long Island with his grandma. A major glitch, however, was that he would only be ten days old.

I figured being a mom hadn't sunk in with me yet. How many mothers of a ten-day old baby would want to ditch him overnight just to dance, shmooze, have cocktails and eat great buffet food? Certainly not Joan, I thought, wincing. But I couldn't help it! Golly, gee! I just really, really wanted to go!

There was only one thing I knew for sure. If it were possible to go, and I decided not to, I would definitely end up feeling resentment towards Jack. I was terrified to experience that, and didn't want the two of us getting off to such a bad start. Particularly if it weren't necessary.

So I locked myself up like a monk, opened the sealed tomes and poured through the gospel of child guidance, seeking some page, some article, even a word that would absolve me of sin for what I was about to do. Surely in ancient times newborns were temporarily bequeathed to the grandmother while the mother was off at some tribal ceremony. But perhaps these modern experts had no patience for the follies of the past.

Then I found it: "Babies should be left with a stranger before they..." Whoops. I'd missed that little word, *never,* right after the *should.* No, all I unearthed was an abundance of potentially unsolvable problems looming before me, despite my enthusiasm for leaving him.

Since he'd been breastfeeding, he might not want to take

a bottle from his grandma. He might not be able to return to breastfeeding after getting used to a bottle. He might throw such a tantrum that we wouldn't be able to leave without feeling remorse. Or he might end up traumatized by this interruption in our intimacy before he'd even formed an attachment to me. Damn. I had my sheets all tied together to sneak out the window of parental responsibility, but Big Mother was watching!

Then I finally found something in the books that gave me hope. They all said in effect: Take your cues from your baby. Each one is different. Let your baby inform you of his needs and limits. It reminded me of the advice I'd read earlier, which I'd already forgotten—to trust my motherly instincts.

So did I have any yet? Well, gosh darn it—maybe I did! None of the problems that friends had mentioned or that I'd read in the books really fit with *my* experience of Jack. I knew him to be such an accepting, agreeable baby. I also knew on a deep level that if he could talk, he would positively insist we go to our friends' wedding. Granted, my experience of him had only been for seven days, but—after all—I *was* his *mother*! So I experimented.

I gave him a bottle of formula. He complied. I observed him day and night in my comings and goings for any signs of separation anxiety. There were none. I followed my instincts and Brian and I went to the wedding.

Upon our return, my mother-in-law said that Jack seemed to regard the two days we were gone as only a slight deviation from the first nine. To my delight, he went back to breastfeeding as if he'd never stopped. This is the way to go, I thought. I like this trusting my instincts! And I really like this kid!

After our trip to Baltimore, I began having difficulty spending all my days alone with Jack, no matter how much of a joy he was to me. I was going stir crazy with cabin fever. Then, when he was three weeks old, my former boss phoned to ask if I wanted to come back to work five hours a day. I had to think for a minute. What mother in America goes back to work when her baby is only three and a half weeks old, unless she really has to? Certainly not Joan—I felt another pang of—what? Could it be anger?

Sure, we could always use the money. But the excitement I felt was coming from imagining myself back on the subway, navigating the buzzing streets alone again, being around my old friends at work—people my own age. I couldn't imagine any other new mother—besides myself—feeling such a thrill at the prospect.

Yet my decision to leave Jack to go to the wedding had turned out well for all of us, and had given me some confidence. Brian worked at night and would be able to watch Jack all day, so we'd be able to split our time equally with him. I could even use a breast pump during my breaks. And I remembered the childcare books encouraging me to take my cues from my baby. Jack was happily gurgling as he watched me on the phone, so after a minute I told my boss, "yes."

I had a strong sense Jack would be fine with the work situation, and I thought I might even end up a better mom for it. I was almost smug when I discovered I was right. My motherly instincts had come through for me once again!

Brian and I soon had the strong urge to go out alone with each other—this after only a few weeks. We wondered if we were different from other parents for wanting it so soon, like we were some kind of perverts. But then I quickly thought about how, when we'd brought Jack to a couple of noisy gatherings with us, he'd happily reached out his arms to everyone. We'd been able to stay late, since Jack had effortlessly fallen asleep in my lap or his bouncy chair or in a bedroom. This seemed to be who he was.

I went ahead and designated Jack a perfect candidate for

babysitting with what I now (so fondly) regarded as my motherly instincts in full force. I thought back to those people who had, during my pregnancy, offered me their time in the future to watch Jack.

I picked up the phone and immediately put it down. What would they think of me? Dashing out to get away from my four-week-old kid when I should be reveling in the opportunity to spend another Family Circle evening bonding with him? It would be easier for me to call and ask someone to bail me out of jail because I'd gone on another PCP-induced shooting spree at the clock tower. That would seem less sacrilegious than abandoning my infant. But again, impending resentment urged me on, and after a few more tries I actually completed the dialing. My friend from work was thrilled at the prospect of watching Jack.

He cried the first time as we left to go out, but we decided to leave anyway. Afterwards I found out what had happened. Just as I suspected, he'd stopped crying after a minute of comforting. From then on, we never again worried about it.

He was five weeks old when he had a second babysitter, a 23-year old friend of mine from work. Xackery had never babysat before, but he'd asked enthusiastically if he could do it. After going over a few basics, I emphasized to him that I never expected a babysitter to be perfect. After all, then he wouldn't be human, and one of our few requirements was for Jack's babysitter to be human.

I viewed Jack's tolerance for being left with other adults not only as a gift to Brian and me, but to Jack, as well—a great opportunity to get to know some of my interesting, funny, kind, unique friends. He even got to experience different mistakes and character flaws than the usual ones he endured with us. I found a lot of relief in that.

For the next six weeks before we left New York, various friends, none of whom happened to have their own children, watched Jack nearly one night a week before he was even two and a half months old. Though he always seemed to have a good time, I still figured I had to be doing something wrong.

I may have liked saying I was "trusting my motherly instincts," but wasn't I really just being thoughtless and indifferent and taking crass advantage of Jack's easygoing nature? What stopped this self-abuse was not my fragile new faith in my instincts, but rather the dread of feeling resentment towards Jack. And thank God for it. But this freedom also led to a period of seeing myself as a "flaky" and depraved mom.

Shuffling between inbox and outbox at work one day, I happened to switch on a parenting radio show just as a call-in mom was asking for advice about taking a class once a week in the evening. The host reproached her for forgetting that being a parent was a responsibility.

Parents, the radio doctor admonished, needed to arrange their schedules so that if one went out on a weekly basis, the other one would be home. And if it weren't possible, she advised the caller to give up the class. It wouldn't be fair to the baby, she said. As if a human being other than the baby's parent would be a negative influence and ruin the kid for life.

Hearing this made me think. Would I have left Jack that often if I thought I was causing him distress? No. A VERY BIG NO. I simply would not have been able to do it. I mean, I'm his *mother* for goodness sake! I left him to go out with Brian knowing in my gut it would be positive and beneficial for all of us.

After having such a strong reaction to the advice, I decided I wasn't such a selfish mother after all. He and I had a great thing going, but we had always worked together *as a team*. Yes, I was my kid's mom, as this talk show host liked to remind her listeners. But Jack was also his mother's son. It takes two to tango, and we'd both been paying a lot of attention. Neither of us had been dancing alone.

Neither had Joan and Graham, I realized. Estranged though we were becoming, Joan and I still reflected each other's inner lives, but now in a more dramatic way—as if she were acting out the Shadow side of my mothering and perhaps I hers. But exhausted and frustrated as she seemed to me, what if she was as plagued by doubt, fear and frustration as I was—only in different ways? Still, when it came to our children's well being, it seemed all was well. Whatever we were over-doing—or under-doing, I was beginning to think it was working for them.

Brian and I soon made plans to move to Los Angeles for various reasons, including careers, living situation, friends. Brian drove all our belongings across the country in a rental truck, and Jack and I took the plane.

"What a well-behaved baby!" a kind balding businessman told me as we got up to leave at the end of the flight to L.A. "You're really doing something right." I told him his nice compliment was undeserved.

Jack was an easy baby—who knows why?—but I definitely hadn't spent any time teaching him at two and a half months the proper way to act on a plane. I thanked the man anyway, and asked him to find a kind word or two for mothers with screaming babies, too, because they probably were doing the best they could. They just weren't as fortunate as I was.

We had to make a quick overnight stop in the East Bay where I had things in storage. I had almost no time to see anyone, so Joan met me at Shur-Gard Storage in El Cerrito for a quick rendezvous.

It was strange to see her for the first time in two years. Each of us now had an extra appendage! She followed me down the labyrinthine corridors to 36B. I opened the door and welcomed her to the ten by ten by ten room filled to the brim with dusty boxes and piles of old furniture.

"I love what you've done with the place!" she crooned. "It's so you!"

"Oh, yes. It's welcoming without being clingy," I grinned. "That's what I was going for. The coziness, the let's be real close friends feeling—"

"But with that piquant zen ambiance of *nothing lasts forever.*"

"Yes, its sooooooooooo transient! I think it really says 'Now.'"

"*Right* now!"

"You know…that's why no windows." I continued. "I had them removed. Nature is so controlling The light always telling you what to do, when to get up, when to eat. It's late. It's early. Yuck! I hate it!"

"I see you don't even *have* a bathroom!"

"Or a kitchen! No external stimuli. No outside pressures," I explained. "No, there's only the present. You can't hang onto the past."

"You just stuff it in boxes."

"Change is all you can count on!" I laughed.

Joan and I always had a hard time stopping once we got going, both of us often preferring the surreal to the real. All the way to Los Angeles, though, that half hour in the storage chamber echoed back at me.

In a way, that room represented what was left of Joan's and my relationship. A fleeting half hour of absolute unadulterated fun left behind in a storage locker. But what if we never come back for it? What if Joan never had room for me in her life again? Well, I'd have to make room. I'd always been the one who phoned—now I'd be the one to drive up and see her. After all, I was the one who had the baby *that wasn't there. I was the lucky one, wasn't I? Lucky.*

Lucky? Soon after arriving in Los Angeles, I forgot what that word even meant. For the next few weeks the only adjectives I used were dark and hopeless ones.

I'd quickly developed a high fever, cold, chills and deep

chest cough. This, while we were living out of suitcases with no place of our own.

The doctor said I might have a virus, but it could also be a bronchial infection, and he offered to give me antibiotics. He said I would have to stop breastfeeding if I took antibiotics, so I decided I had a virus instead. After various herbal and home remedies I only got worse, but like a cholera-ravaged peasant in a Siberian ice cave, I kept on breastfeeding.

We were camped out at my friend Cynthia's during that time, and on one of those wretched evenings she came home to find me sitting in a dark corner, too miserable to even switch on a lamp. My body, like a rigid statue, was back-lit in pallid green. My eyes stared down at the floor.

I'd been in my nightgown all day, and I was too depressed to notice if it was time for squirming, slurping Jack to be switched to the other breast. I probably looked to her like a wet nurse who'd just been shot in the back of the head.

"Brian said he'd be back from Thrifty Drugs five minutes ago," I coughed out in despair. It had been ten minutes, so I naturally assumed he was dead.

Jack nursed away despite my sudden bursts of shivering and wheezing. I was too weak to actually hold him, but he was clinging like a monkey, lustily sucking the last bit of life out of me. I gazed up at Cynthia, and I knew I looked a wreck. But worse, I thought she could see the resentment I was beginning to feel towards my own son—even before I could face it myself.

Brian had been a great help until he got sick. Then Jack followed suit. The sweet little cherub I'd known and appreciated so much suddenly disappeared. I guess it had to happen sometime.

I was up every night with Jack, the two of us feverish and coughing and gagging and sneezing. I was frightened by Jack's extreme crankiness, his difficulty breathing, his glazed eyes and the cough of a fifty-year old man. Sure, we'd been to a pediatrician, and I was giving him droppers of pink antibiotic glop, but what was really the best way for me to help him? I had no idea.

Where were my instincts now, when I needed them? Where were his for that matter? He cried all the time, so his crying specified nothing to me anymore. He was too sick to let me know what he needed. And I was too sick to know if I'd even be able to take care of him.

Then it hit me. What if Jack had been a colicky baby, or chronically ill, or more difficult all around? I remembered what Joan had been through with Graham's colic—how many times she'd felt powerless and desperate. She had exhausted all her motherly instincts getting absolutely nowhere. Like I was now.

So knowing full well it meant Jack's breastfeeding would have to come to an end, I made the decision—without any instincts, insight, or (what felt like) even a brain—to go back to the doctor and try the antibiotics. I'd always been aware of the many advantages a baby got from breastfeeding. But that was irrelevant. I just couldn't take feeling sick one more day. Period. End of story. Or so I thought.

A few days later we all seemed a slight bit better, so the three of us went out to look for a place to live. We were desperate to have a home.

The woman who managed one of the nicer apartments we looked at had a toddler and a baby on the way. "Are you breast-feeding?" she asked me out of the blue. I assumed she was, and that she thought I should be, too. I immediately made her into an authority figure.

She had such a perfect haircut. There was a beautiful black piano with a book open to classical music. She'd even put a toddler gate up in her one-story apartment.

"I've been sick," I told her. "My ribs ache from coughing. I still have chills. I stopped so I could take antibiotics, and I guess now the milk's gone."

"You really should call the La Leche League," she said. "I have their phone number. I just read the research, and babies who aren't breastfed the first year have lower IQ points as children. I have the name of the journal somewhere. The women at La Leche can explain how to get your milk back and it shouldn't be hard."

Obviously, she thought I should stay sick a little longer and stop the antibiotics. I thought the whole thing was kind of ridiculous, but then she mentioned the difference in the number of IQ points. I immediately repressed it. It was something huge—like twelve.

Jack and I had communicated so well up to the time we'd become sick. But what was I supposed to do now about this IQ business, without any instincts or brain?

If only Jack would cry out something to me! Anything! *Get me back on the breast milk, Ma! Goddamnit! You want me to grow up a moron?*

I'd obviously been intimidated by this woman. So as soon as I got home I made the call. I remembered Joan really liking La Leche, telling me how supportive and nonjudgmental they were. So I wasn't surprised to be greeted by such a warm, down-to-earth voice. The friendly Leaguer told me what I'd have to do to get the milk back. She explained quite nonchalantly what my rigorous schedule would be each day grinding away at the breast pump. But I was still feeling lousy. We still had no place to live. To me the whole process sounded like a gargantuan task, possibly tolerable if I'd been wearing a bell around my neck and answered to the name Elsie. What I was starting to realize was that when I didn't want to do something, I really *didn't want to do it.*

I was still feeling lousy. We still had no place to live. Was I willing to take the chance the research was wrong? That wasn't really the question.

I don't think IQ points mattered much to me. Had science ever proved IQ to be the primary predictor of a fulfilling and meaningful life? But that was just my opinion. I had another person to consider. Maybe those IQ points would be a big deal to Jack. Would he be at the therapist's office years from now, believing my selfish decision years before had kept him out of Yale? I doubted that. It was too inane.

My motherly instincts were slowly returning, telling me to give up breastfeeding for good. My old but helpful fear had returned to guide me. What truly made me stick with the bottle was that recurring image of myself at Cynthia's in the dark, nursing Jack—the seeds of undeserved resentment towards him starting to take root.

Sometimes parents don't have a choice. We may just have to continue doing something good for our children, even though it's bad for us. And that can sometimes make us resentful—a feeling, that is for me the most painful of all, like a hatchet in the back of my head.

But in my breastfeeding dilemma I was not trapped. I had a choice. Just as I'd had when I'd gone to the wedding, returned to work, and spent an evening out.

I don't think I chose the option the experts would have recommended. But was I only supposed to use my motherly instincts to prevent my child's suffering and not my own? Was it so wrong to consider a solution that also took into account my own well-being?

Back when I was being bottle-fed, breast-feeders were the weirdos. The dogma-doo was simply on the other foot. Maybe it isn't really *which* decisions are made that matters—but how they are made. Blind obedience to tradition is just as silly as blind obedience to science.

I wouldn't mind if some of my instinct for self-consideration rubbed off on Jack, either genetically or through my influence. I'd like him to feel it's all right to consciously question the rules and to give his own well-being equal weight in his decision-making.

"But boys don't suffer from any lack of self-interest." So says our cultural myth of manhood. But is that true? Don't we all sacrifice parts of ourselves in order to fit in and do what's expected?

Men may lose out on a rich emotional life, women on self-determination. Social dictates have made us all a bit one-sided. And the one thing I wanted for Jack was for him to be himself—all of himself. Even if it meant wishing upon him all the conflicts that came with it.

Six years later, I'd forgotten all about my little war between the Bottle and the Breast. Jack was excited to go to "Big School" and he hit first grade running—reading *Harry Potter* by midyear and flying through his math workbooks. I was delighted, of course, but not because I felt an academically-oriented child was "better." As an admittedly lazy mom, I rejoiced in the fact that if he had an easier time of it, so would I.

If I had indeed beaten down his intelligence with the bottle, those minus twelve points didn't seem to be ruining his life. Maybe he'd been keeping a few points in reserve, just for emergencies—like for helping him understand a mom like me.

SINGLE MOTHERHOOD REVISITED

(or the Gray Divorcée)

in which Joan puts herself under house arrest...

Linda could cycle through more emotional extremes in an hour than the entire population of Italy could in a year. In fact she'd probably invented a few new ones. But when it came to her opinions she was a rock of moderation. She could always come up with a dozen alternative explanations to my conspiracy theories.

"Don't you think Lockheed's CEO's are really just like us?" she would suggest gently. "They're probably too busy making warheads to be interfering with your tax refund." Whether it was personal or political, it was just human beings doing what human beings do.

That's why I could tell Linda anything. She was incapable of blaming me. She lived by the credo: Every experience is valid. When my marriage went down in flames, I needed Linda. Badly.

But it was the Old Linda I wanted. The vulnerable, needy Linda, so rich with problems and flaws. And so radically non-judgmental. I wasn't sure the New Linda would be so understanding of my failings—the now competent, stable Linda who seemed to be handling motherhood and wifedom with such aplomb.

How could I admit to someone who seemed to be doing everything right that I had ruined my "perfect" marriage. Just an accidental stifled gasp of disapproval from Linda would hit me now like a shaming tirade from anyone else. Her opinion carried too much weight with me. And I was too close to the edge. On the other hand, she might take it too lightly because— after all, hadn't I been a single mother most of my life? What was the big deal?

I *had* been a single mother before, but that first time I'd chosen it. I should have seen this one coming, though. I'd known that Thom was miserable.

The only reason Thom hadn't left me already was Graham. As he held his weary head in his hands one night, I urged him to divorce me. But he'd always been so dependent on routine, so averse to change, I guess I didn't really think he'd do it.

Then it happened. He wanted to "talk."

I could imagine him offering his Official Resignation with the tear-choked farewell of a shattered man—torn between spouse and sanity. But Thom was giddy with excitement as he gave me the boot, chattering away about his plans for a new life like a kid off to Disneyland.

Well, hadn't I always wanted him to be fulfilled? I wasn't about to rain on his parade, so I tried to be supportive and enthusiastic. "Good for you, Thom. Go for it! How can I help?"

A few days later I was putting up a picket fence around the old fixer-upper we'd just bought, trying to channel my pain into hammering. Thom had been planning to design one himself, but I got impatient. When Thom came by to move some more of his things out, he stared at the fence. Then the mild-mannered David Banner snapped and out busted a geeky Hulk, bellowing about how I was doing it all wrong. As I watched him rant, a searing memory of our *Talk* cut through me like a scythe. What had I been thinking? *Go for it, Thom? How can I help, Thom?*

I dropped my shovel and hung my head in the hot sun, dripping sweat and tears. I wanted to get down on my knees and beg him to forgive me, to love me again, to stay—like something out of a bad Bette Davis movie. I looked up to see him stomp into the house so he could do more leaving.

The next day he returned to rip out my posts and dig his own holes. He poured the cement and stormed off. The posts were now positioned just a bit too far apart for the picket fencing to fit, so I had to dig them all up again and start over. But the whole thing seemed justifiable to me. In my mind, the fence debacle was a microcosm of our marriage—how I'd crashed through Thom's boundaries one too many times. If only a post-hole-digger could resurrect our relationship. But there were too many if-only's. The past was lost, the future unimaginable, and the present, only an aftermath of obsessive review.

It was because of me, I thought, that Graham was fatherless. And since I hadn't made any friends yet who might have been able to dispute that claim, I put my shoulder to the wheel of a well-oiled self-recrimination mill.

For the first six months it was one long anxiety attack. How would my son—this not so adaptable child—be able to handle life with a single mother? My first two children had already been through it—the Domino Effect of Divorce. First you lose the dad, then the house, and then the car. Then the dryer gives out, followed by the washer, the TV, and the vacuum cleaner until the "FREE—TAKE ALL" roadside piles become your shopping mall.

We moved forty times in twenty years (no wonder Tim at first mistook his calling for real estate). And if the bill-paying roulette and Repo Man raids weren't depressing enough, there was always that end-of-the-month panic of opening the cupboard and wondering how we'd make it till payday on cornflakes, baking soda and Metamucil. It wasn't deprivation so much as aggravation.

My latchkey kids were home alone till I got off my day job. During our few moments of togetherness, I would inevitably coerce one of them to run lines with me for some era-hopping play about morphing Victorian transsexuals. Then, promising it would all be different when I made it big, I'd drag them off to sleep on the floor of whatever theatre I was cleaning that night.

But I also remembered the day I overheard my fifteen year-old son bouncing a ball with his sister against the side of our cramped one-bedroom apartment. "I'm glad I didn't have it easy," he told her. "I think it made me a better person." Still, I wasn't eager to raise another better person at that price.

Soon winter came to our new old house with the broken heater. The relentless arctic cold seemed to confirm my failure as a mother. I couldn't even get the "providing shelter" part right. Then the holidays released the rage beneath my anxiety. It seemed to burst out of me from nowhere—I couldn't prevent it or control it. And Graham was a convenient target. After the outbursts subsided, I would try to atone.

But how does an ogre make amends? I couldn't bear to add insult to injury with endless apologies—especially when he might still be feeling afraid of me, so I decided to use a mediator.

Graham and I had often carried on conversations through his beloved bald sock horse, Girlfriend. Through meticulous instruction and tireless correction, he had trained me to speak for Girlfriend in a high lilting whisper, a voice incompatible with malevolence.

With her Marilyn Monroe breathiness dancing on the air, Girlfriend went to work, verbalizing the feelings a four-year old couldn't articulate, scolding Mommy and explaining the way she'd better act next time. But if this helped Graham at all, I don't know. It didn't assuage my guilt. Still, I had to let him know it was my fault—not his.

Even after the Yuletide raging passed, I kept wondering if "They" would take Graham away from me. After all, shouldn't they?

Stewart took the train up to comfort me. He read his latest poems, showed me a documentary on Kandinski, and played our old Elton John favorites on the piano. Somewhere in the back corner of my head—where my brain wasn't completely beaten into submission by remorse—I knew he was being terribly charming and funny. But he might as well have been entertaining a panel of aluminum siding. He didn't mind, but I felt awful. I was a bad wife, an unforgivable mother and a worthless friend to boot.

I needed counseling desperately, but there wasn't enough money to put gas in the car, and after awhile there wasn't any car to put gas into. So I turned to digging. I spent that spring slamming my shovel into the ground. A chain gang of one. At first it was a garden. Then I "terraced" the back hill. Well, I dug some very large grave-shaped pits. Archaeological dig or self-internment? I wasn't sure.

As I did my penance, Graham played with his duckling. For weeks I let Ducky Dane spend the night next to our bed. Sometimes I felt that duck was a little Rock of Gibraltar providing the security that neither of his parents could offer in those terrible months.

Thom had taken a job in another city, so Graham didn't see him for awhile. He could accept Daddy working far away. But I didn't know how to help him understand what was really happening without doing him more emotional harm. Dozens of classes and workshops and a hundred books on child development hadn't taught me how to handle *this* divorce with *this* child at *this* age. I was stumped.

Instead of using the word, divorce, which I felt incompetent to define for him, I offered the vapid story that Mommy and Daddy were not able to make their decisions together anymore, and married people needed to do that. Our separation would allow us to make our own decisions. God, it sounded so *You do your thing and I'll do mine.* Was a stupid free love platitude from the 60's any match for his emotional apocalypse now?

"Daddy will always love you. You didn't do anything to make Daddy leave," I said with the authority of a junior college textbook and about as much warmth. On I stumbled. "Daddy needs to live away from Mommy. He wishes he could still live with you." It sounded pathetically contrived. I wondered how much of this made any sense to him.

Children deserved honesty, but claiming full responsibility for ruining my marriage didn't seem right. At four years old, Graham didn't see himself as entirely separate from me. If I portrayed myself as the "bad one," wasn't it possible that Graham would identify with that "badness?" And if I put it in terms of a mistake I'd made, wouldn't he naturally assume that one day he could make a mistake that Daddy would never forgive?

I was certainly not going to tell him his father didn't love me anymore. Then I would have to explain that husband-wife love was not as durable as parent-child love. And how would Graham make heads or tails of that? There was only one kind of love as far as he knew. Therefore, if one love relationship could be killed, then all love must be fragile and temporary. Sooner or later he would hear about the very popular god of conditional love who rewarded the obedient and scorched the rest. But for now, I felt he was entitled to believe in unconditional love. I wasn't about to mess with that.

Well, why not a nice healing allegory? Sure! A compulsive queen depletes the king's treasury of magic turnips, which turns her husband into a toad. He leaves his son a giant promise turnip before he sets off to—No. A little too real.

Every approach to the subject of divorce—no matter how

practical, spiritual or developmentally appropriate, had its unacceptable downside. Like Rock, Paper and Scissors in a mad philosophical Ro-Sham-Bo. Honesty beats platitude; platitude beats allegory; allegory beats honesty!

If only our marriage had been fraught with yelling or name-calling, I might have been able to say, "See? Daddy and Mommy are happier now that we aren't together fighting all the time!" But Thom and I had rarely even raised our voices, except to laugh. Our family had not exploded. It had evaporated. How could Graham ever fathom this quiet, civilized dissipation of life as he'd known it?

After months of scalding in the crucible of post-marital remorse, I heard from Thom that he was moving back to the area. I was saved! Graham would get to see his daddy on a regular basis. That would be good for Thom too. Never confident as a father, he was overwhelmed in his new role as a visiting parent. I thought closer proximity would help everyone feel more comfortable. But it wasn't that simple for Graham.

He couldn't go to his father's house without getting sick. What seemed to me to be a child's natural insecurity would have been all the proof needed to convict me in family court of alienating a child from its father. The cry of "Alienator" was becoming as surefire, popular and ridiculous a charge as "Lesbian" had been when my first two children were young. But luckily, Thom was his old easy-going self again, and we worked around Graham's ambivalence until it disappeared about a year later.

I began to realize how lucky I was to have married a man who would make such a fine ex-husband. There was none of the gunplay, kidnapping and restraining order hoopla that high-lighted my first divorce. It was a Hallmark card version of joint custody.

Thom and I had remained united in regard to what we considered best for Graham. We both had a similar—if unorthodox—vision. The first time Graham caught a ball we were thrilled, of course. But a few years later, when he sat riveted in front of *"Invasion of the Body Snatchers"* we were *ecstatic*.

We were so comfortably united in our parenting, in fact, that I sometimes forgot we weren't married anymore. Even after Thom had a girlfriend, I was still wearing my wedding ring and calling him "Honey." When I finally pulled that ring off, it wasn't because I could finally let go. I was just sick of advertising my denial.

Graham should have the ring, I thought, as I nestled it into a velvet-lined box. "This can be for your wife someday," I told him through my tears. A week later it was lost, a cosmic kick in the pants from some exasperated middle management deity.

I knew Linda must have been shocked to hear my voice on the phone, but all she expressed was delight.

"A Girlfriend? Thom?"

"Yes. With a daughter. Very nice, both of them." I was in a hurry to get to the nightmare part. "He's been taking Graham with them to the beach and on overnights and—"

"Thom?"

"Yes, Thom. I mean when did he ever—EVER—spend time with us? Now he's suddenly playing daddy to *her* kid. I let him have it. It took me five phone calls to get it all said."

"Of course."

"Well, his stupid machine kept cutting me off."

"Ohhhhh. . . So what's with this girlfriend."

"Jane?"

"Okay, we'll call her Jane. Is that why he left? I mean how long had he been seeing her?"

"Oh no. That's not why. I told you. It was my fault."

"You had a—?"

"No, I never—" I sucked in a quick breath and shot it out like a poison arrow: "I spentallhismoney."

She was silent. Oh dear, now that I'm finally reconnecting

with her, she probably doesn't want anything to do with the complete sociopath I've become.

At last she spoke. "You're sure you spent *all* his money?" she probed gently as if I'd just confessed to watching daytime TV instead of grand larceny, her subdued skepticism ringing out loud and clear. Linda The History Major was a stickler for accuracy, but I knew she was asking for more than facts. She wondered if I would really condemn myself right in front of her. I accepted the challenge.

"Thirty thousand dollars I still owe him."

She paused. "Is that a lot?" This was her standard response whenever I spoke in numeric values instead of feelings. Against my own will, I relaxed. "Well. It's a lot to Thom." I exhaled, suddenly feeling exhausted. "You know I always thought of myself as an embezzler. Now I'm thinking what I did was extortion."

"Hmmm."

"He never gave me his time, so maybe unconsciously I was punishing him. God. I am crazy." Certainly now she would have to condemn me. Either for my actions or for their motivation.

"Well," she said, still refusing to take the bait, "time *is* money."

"Yeah, maybe it—"

"But I bet he recovered. He got the two houses, didn't he? And the car? You pay him rent. In Monopoly that means he wins."

I let out a breath held in for three years. Oh my god, the relief! Yes! Maybe two houses and a car could ease his pain (and my shame). I melted, wishing I'd been able to talk to her about this years earlier. I was opening my mouth to gush some sentimental blather when I heard her call out to someone, "It's ready? Okay. I'll be right there." And then back to me—like a child called in from play, "I gotta go. Sorry. Bye." Click. I don't know why that sent a chill down my spine. Maybe because it reminded me of one of those polygamist wives who turned into a pumpkin if she wasn't home cooking dinner by four o'clock. No, my reaction was probably more personal.

The family dinner table thing was something Thom and I had found useful only for dredging up repressed memories better left repressed, so we happily dispensed with it. But that didn't mean everyone should.

I knew Brian. If there was an ideal, relaxed husband, he was it. But Linda? Rushing to the dinner table to play the role of nuclear wife? Was she actually taking to this domestic stuff that had always been anathema to her? Okay, Brian cooked—true, but she was playing her part quite convincingly.

What timing! Just as I was beginning to enjoy my freedom from constant concern over a partner's wishes, Linda the Me-Queen seemed to be bending over backwards to fit into the traditional family routine. But why was I uncomfortable with it? If she was happy...But was she? Oh come on, was I actually worried about Linda lapsing in her duty to put Linda first? No, I was probably annoyed at getting a taste of my own medicine. I remembered how she'd felt when I hung up on her because a little man demanded my complete attention.

But I didn't really feel snubbed. Linda was the One-Minute-Shame-Buster, and she'd given her usual hundred and fifty percent, putting my crime in better perspective and rolling out the red carpet of unconditional acceptance.

I sighed again. I knew I had a lot more sighs to go. I felt as if Linda had released the north wind chained up by the old witch in the Kalavala tales. Yes, maybe I'd been exonerated. I couldn't help smiling. The house, the car, the 401 K. It was a toe-tapping ditty of restitution. And then the question floated before me like a game show challenge.

"And Joan, what will you take in this divorce settlement? The car or the house? Or maybe the other house? How about your share of his 401 K?" I was beginning to sweat when a husky voice urged me to 'Take it all, Girl!" And there was Chinette, baby on hip, twin toddlers climbing her thighs, and a pregnant belly bulging above hip-huggers. The sliver of over-stuffed bra marked a sort of demarcation line between mating call and response. "Have you ever heard of community property, Hon?"

"Oh, no. See, that doesn't really apply. He bought everything. I never had an outside job during the marriage. I just took care of Graham. And bankrupted us."

"Well, I guess that answers my question." She tossed an open carton of Lady Kents between the toddlers and they pounced like tiger cubs. "But do you think I could afford a sitter for my baker's dozen and a little extra for the dog races if I hadn't gone to court a few times?"

"Oh, we didn't have to go to court! We did it ourselves with that NoLo book."

"Yeah. I can tell."

I slumped into the disheveled couch next to the dog. Linda had lifted a weight from my shoulders and I didn't really want to replace it with another one labeled "sucker." Who could say for sure who was at fault in this *Rashomon* divorce. So, rather than try to find objective truth where there probably was none, I settled for a luxurious soak in the tub of *absolution*. My debt had been paid. My criminal activity did not seem so criminal anymore. Over the next few months the depression abated, and my life began to chug forward.

Ah, the old familiar autonomy of single parenthood! Even if I envied Linda her stable marriage to a nifty husband, I didn't miss the stressful compromises of being part of a couple. And that welcome detachment helped me begin to see my ex-husband in a new light.

Throughout our marriage I'd always nagged him to quit his steady but unbearable job and follow his heart. But Thom was not one to jump into the unknown like I was. Now I could see how beneficial this constancy was for Graham. To have a dependable man to count on. As unsure as I was about his motives toward me, it was easy to see he was trying to do right by Graham.

Thom took plenty of abuse from his friends for that paternal commitment. "And it's strange," he said one day at Graham's favorite taco place. "It's never the men." He was painstakingly folding his napkin like an army bed for morning inspection, until it formed a snug origami cocoon around his burrito. "It's always a woman harassing me about why my 'lazy ex doesn't get off her butt and stop mooching off me.'"

A rocket blast of hot sauce shot out from my poorly-torn packet, landing with a splat on his sleeve (I'd already soiled my own blouse, as usual). He rubbed at the stain as if it were the very essence of my demonic boundary issues. "I'm sorry. I'm sorry!" I wanted to ram my apology down his throat!

Graham suddenly spit out the bite of tortilla he'd taken. I patted him on the back. He hadn't been able to handle solid food for six months—ever since he'd choked at a restaurant and I'd had to give him the Heimlich maneuver. So I'd been delighted when he'd said he wanted a quesadilla this morning. Even if he couldn't eat it, at least he'd wanted to give it a try.

Graham let out a long groan as he put his head in his hands, then ran off to the kids' area.

"You know, as a husband," Thom picked up where he left off, "if you can afford a stay-at-home wife you're a hero. But if your ex-wife can afford to stay home with your kid, you're a shlump."

I nodded, hovering over my taco as if I were defusing a bomb. Sharing your husband's salary so you could raise your child at home was a saintly sacrifice. Scraping by on child support so you could *remain* a stay-at-home mother—was being a leech. How illogical! And yet, hadn't I always felt guilty for "mooching" off Thom—married or divorced?

"It's funny," Thom puzzled between tiny, fastidious bites. "You're not supposed to be a deadbeat dad, but people think you're crazy not to ditch the first kid and run off to make another one with some young bimbo."

Graham was back.

"Too noisy in there?" Thom, unruffled by Graham's repertoire of sensitivities, handed him one of the liquid-meals-in-a-can I'd brought along just in case he couldn't manage chewing. Then with the enthusiasm of an armchair anthropologist Thom went on about how this curious dump-the-old/breed-the-new phenomenon must be rooted in the same instinct for genetic survival that drives a lion to kill all the cubs when he takes over a new pride. "Or," he sighed, "maybe women just want my money."

Yeah, I was glad Graham had a dad who paid child support, but it went deeper than that.

Thom wasn't the active kind of father who wrestled with his son or took him fishing, but he offered Graham something I felt was more important—an acceptance of who he was, and an interest in who he was becoming. The fact the Graham didn't like organized sports or want to join Cub Scouts didn't faze him. Graham didn't have to do anything or be anything to please Thom or gain his approval.

My relationship with Thom began to look a lot like it had before we were married, perhaps because my expectations had fallen away. Now that he was my ex, I no longer made the assumptions I would make about a husband. The borders around our separate selves were clear, and I was doing my best to stay within mine.

I wished Graham could have learned about healthy relationships from watching his own parents as a married couple in action. But at least he could still see us working things out together once in a while. Even if they weren't big things—just sharing the power tools or making plans to repair the house or even talking about old science fiction films. After awhile we were spending more time together as a "broken family" than when we'd lived together. I was grateful. For Graham's sake I wanted this divorce to work. Maybe Thom and I had failed at marriage. But as ex-spouses, we were doing a hell of a job.

MIRROR MIRROR ON THE WALL

(or The Fraidy-Cat Factor)

*in which Linda discovers Jack isn't
the beanstalk-climbing type...*

I didn't hear about Joan's divorce for six months. And then it was only three words: "It's my fault." I kept calling, but she was always too depressed to talk.

Eventually she humored me with a thirty-second snapshot of the whole thing, out-of-focus and badly framed with her head chopped off, after which she just breathed heavily into the phone till I went away. As glad as I was to finally hear from her, our brief contact aroused my too accessible feelings of rejection. I couldn't understand why someone would cut herself off from friends to stay buried in pain.

Could talking to me have been that much more unpleasant than hiding away inside her lonely, bottled-up, stressed-out life? I missed her so much I wanted to slap her. I suppose I really did understand, though. Depression just works that way. But it was easier to get mad at *her* than at a mental illness.

Then it happened. Two years later. *She* called *me*. She'd come out of her fetal position and was actually able to insert that little word *not* between "It was" and "all my fault."

I tried to praise her efforts. "That's great, Joan. But you sound like Bill Clinton, and he's still way too contrite. You both need more practice." She barked out one cracking bleat. Her laugh was rusty.

For a moment I sympathized with Thom. He'd probably done the best he could. Joan didn't need a husband; she needed a wrangler.

She talked to me for a whole ten minutes that day. Mostly about Graham. How would he adjust to having a single mother? And from what I knew of Graham being so sensitive to everything, maybe it would be tough.

Even if I had to throw Jack in the back of the car and speed back to New York, he would probably take it all in stride. Jack was so different from Graham, so independent and flexible. I was lucky. Parenting didn't create the double bind it did with Joan.

Sure, I was Jack's mom, but in sort of an informal-treaty way. For Joan it seemed more like a Biosphere experiment. Jack, thank heaven, seemed to get many of his needs met without my even noticing. As if by osmosis. But that began to worry me. What if he got *other* things by osmosis?

When I first met Joan, she was living in Santa Cruz where her older son, Tim, had become an avid surfer. I asked her once if she'd ever tried it. "God no," she said, "I'm terrified of the ocean." That made a big impression on me about how much—or really how little—influence we have over our kids.

A frightened mother doesn't necessarily make a frightened child. What a relief! If Joan could have sane children, maybe I could too!

It was only a few months later that I began to notice a shocking change in Jack's behavior. My little easy-going take-everywhere do-everything kid was becoming a bundle of nerves. He wouldn't look at strangers, couldn't do anything without me, wouldn't let go of my leg. My anxiety began to grow, as much as I tried to hide it. Then, suddenly I thought of Joan! She'd been raising a fearful child herself for a few years now. Who better to help me with Jack's new over-dependency?

I decided to give her a call. After blurting out a few of the essentials, she gave me one of her comforting uh-huhs and I relaxed.

"See, it's not that I don't want him to be scared. It's just so new for me and I mean, he won't do anything without me now. I guess you know what that's like!"

"Yes," she answered, a little too serenely. "He wants your protection." *She does know something I don't.*

"Oh, my protection. Okay. From what?"

"The pressures of the world. All that stimulation."

"Yeah, exactly! That's why I called you. My friends want to take him to Disneyland."

"Oh. Disneyland. I hate that place!" Was that a smug chuckle in her voice?

"Yeah," I giggled. "I know I could never take him."

"Of course you couldn't. I think it's great you're sheltering him from something so spiritually inappropriate."

As she droned on about how the media is murdering our children's souls, my blood boiled.

I wasn't sheltering him! I *wanted* him to go to Disneyland, and I was frustrated he might resist this terrific opportunity. I would never be able to take him there, myself—not without an economy-sized bottle of Valium. Brian and I both hated theme parks. That's why I'd been thrilled when my friends invited him to go during Spring Break. But now I was so angry at Joan's sanctimonious edict, I wanted to drag him off to Disneyland right now, kicking and screaming! What had come over her? I forced out a bitter thank you and told her I had to go.

This fear thing with our kids was something we actually had in common, but she had to play Mother Superior with me. Every kid should get to go to Disneyland. Maybe Joan disapproved, but in my unenlightened viewpoint it was more spiritually appropriate that kids have a lot of fun!

The only problem was Jack. He didn't want to do anything fun anymore.

He refused to go to kids' birthday parties unless I was right there next to him, so he could hold my hand and cling to me. Then it was fine for him.

Sometimes he'd spend over an hour just sitting in my lap. If I were lucky, there might be a five-minute window before the end where he felt comfortable enough to run around with the other kids and I could breathe a little. But mostly we sat huddled together in some noisy Chucky Cheese, watching the other kids play and scream.

I prayed this was a phase he was going through, because the idea of being stuck with a clingy child was about as attractive as watching an *Arrowsmith* concert in a stadium of sweaty hash-heads, nude. I tried not to show him it bothered me, as I held my breath and waited for him to snap out of it.

But he wasn't snapping. He wouldn't even go on a merry-go-round. I told him he could sit on my lap and we'd ride on one of those benches that didn't go up and down. "No," he said. "Too scary."

Pony rides were out, too. Even where the ponies were chained in a circle and look drugged on Quaaludes. Even if I promised to continuously call out, "Look! Mommy's right here!" He was too afraid.

He wouldn't swing on monkey bars or go down the slide— no matter how gentle the slope. Way too frightening.

He wouldn't ride on the kiddie train, even if he could sit on my lap. "Not ever!" he said, as if he were fed up with having such an irresponsible mom, and having to be the one to protect us both from getting ourselves killed.

He just didn't want to have fun. I know this because of the many times I asked him: "Don't you want to have fun? Well?" His answer was always the same: "No. I don't want to."

So what exactly did he want to do? He didn't want to leave and go to a movie or a children's museum or home to watch TV. All he wanted was to sit and stare with fascination at the other kids as they played, many of them younger and smaller than he was.

So together we sat, watching them climb, ride and laugh themselves silly with pleasure. Jack's timidity really bothered me, and though I didn't like my reaction to it, I couldn't seem to stop judging him.

I didn't dream of Jack becoming an astronaut or deep sea diver. But I was a huge baseball fan, and I had hoped to go to a Little League game someday and watch Jack steal second base. That didn't seem to be where we were headed.

In the neighborhood, in his pre-school, at the park, going through the checkout line at Trader Joe's, my antenna has always selected out any chatter having the potential to make me feel worse. Back then it was: "Your daughter has no fear. How great!" or "My son's a real go-getter—he just jumps up there and does it!" or "She falls down all the time, but then she picks herself up and goes right back at it!"

I wondered if anyone would be interested in hearing, "Jack falls down all the time, and then he cries and doesn't want to play anymore!" What could someone say to that? *"It's OK, he'll change!"*

My wonderfully anonymous little Everyman, Jack—named after the fella who let you have the parking space, the guy who waved from the train for no reason, the whistling doorman who called you "lovely" —my little Jack, who'd always seemed to float like a happy rainbow around my life now stood in the middle of it like a forty pound Rubic's cube. He had a real name now. He was "The Jack That Wouldn't."

Eventually, more well-intentioned words were offered: "I think Jack's getting braver!" or "He seems a little more assertive! Good!" or "He's been jumping into things more lately! Hasn't he?" Extremely innocent comments, I thought. So why was listening to them such a problem for me? Because I took it to mean something was wrong with him and needed to be improved.

Yet his being more cautious than rambunctious had always made it easy for me to take him to adult get-togethers, made it pleasant for other adults to be around him. But now that caution had reached critical mass. And I knew what lay ahead. His fear would be his ruin. No question.

Those compliments he got for becoming more courageous made me want to cheer him on: *Be more confident, Jack! More aggressive and feisty! Forge ahead, Sweetie! Do it for me, OK? Don't you want to make it in America? If you're a wimp, you're gonna end up a loser!*

That was what worried me. I didn't think America would stand and wait for "less adventurous" kids like Jack. What happened to kids like him when they grew up? I imagined they could easily be ignored, or stepped upon, or left to do all the menial break-your-back jobs for the go-getter types. Was I being too ridiculous and fearful myself?

I decided Jack's fear had everything to do with his not being logical. I took him back to L.A.'s Griffith Park and the pony ride, pointing out to him the sweet faces and big kind eyes of the horses, explaining how they were really more like old gray mares—so dull and lumbering they would never want to hurt anyone. Even if they wanted to, they wouldn't know how to do it! Right? "So Jack," I asked him. "Whatdya' say? Don't you want to have fun?"

"No."

"Are you sure?"

"Well, uh..."

"OK! You'll see, it'll be fun! It's great you want to try it!"

For as long as I live, I will never forget Jack's face as I watched from behind the gate that kept parents from racing out and rescuing their kids. Around the circle he came on that plodding horse, his cheeks red and soaked with tears; his eyes, nose, mouth squished together in a screaming cry of pain: "MOMMY!"

I should have been flogged and humiliated in public at the very least. It was all my fault. How wrong I'd been to push him! That's when it hit me—the flashback that opened my eyes.

I remembered a shameful night back in the fourth grade. My mom had dropped me off at a Halloween party at the home of one of my classmates. The crashing thunder, flashes of lightning and rivers of rain that night were frightening enough, but the family had also turned their home into a haunted house—black walls, waving flashlights, scary noises, giant spider webs and monsters jumping out of corners. At least that's what I heard later, since I never actually went in myself. I had a panic attack instead.

I couldn't stop shaking. I thought I was going to die. Simply hearing about the haunted house was enough to do me in. In fact, I have to admit I *still* get scared when I think about that place. But I was the only kid there who was terrified.

I asked the girl's mother, with much embarrassment, if I could call my mom and have her come get me. My mom was at the front door in twenty minutes.

Of course, at school on Monday, I had to endure my classmates telling me how much FUN they'd had, and what was wrong with me? Why did I have to go home so early? It made me feel so different from them. All the other kids knew how to have fun. I only knew was how to be afraid. And I was already nine years old!

For much of my life, my mother—God rest her soul—could be very domineering with her opinions about how I should and shouldn't be. However, in this situation she was completely understanding. Not to take away credit, but I don't think her supportiveness came from enlightened parenting. It just never bothered her if I was afraid. In fact, she loved it when I turned to her and she felt needed.

She was an immigrant who came to this country as a child in 1920, a refugee from the wars in Poland. Her past made her fearful of many things, but that part of herself never seemed to bother her much, and she never tried to change it. After all, she had turned into a 1950's American woman, and fearfulness in women was assumed, if not condoned outright. Besides, she had my father (at least in her mind) to protect her from the world's demons. Having grown up during the "liberated" 60's and 70's myself, I knew that no man—including my husband— could protect me from the world's demons. Godamnit!

How clear it all seemed now. Jack's "problem" was really mine. I've always been the fearful type, and he gets it from *me!*

Although the Halloween party incident stands out most in my memory, I had many other experiences of faint-heartedness throughout my childhood. And as an adult I've seen myself as more sensitive than most, and afraid more often than almost anyone else I knew.

But unlike my mother who lived in a different time, it's been nearly impossible for me to accept my sheepish side, and I've spent a lifetime fighting it. That's obviously why similar qualities in Jack have been hard for me to embrace.

I recently read a quote by the comic, Sid Caesar. It was about how once you retire, you say, 'OK, the argument's over.' You're not mad at anybody, especially yourself. Once you make friends with yourself, life becomes wonderful. In Sid's words, I'm finally beginning to make friends with myself, except the argument isn't over, and I'm still in the thick of it. Can I ever accept the cowardly side of me?

It's hard when fearfulness gets little respect from the culture we live in. Maybe our fears remind others of the vulnerability they'd like to deny or repress. I think fear sometimes has a lot to say and in many situations it deserves to be listened to.

Is there room in America for those of us, who, at certain times see no choice but to give in to our anxiety and apprehension? Or must we be looked at with disdain? Is the spotlight only for those who continuously conquer their fear?

"Come on, the rocks are so close together!" I said to Jack. The stones across the shallow creek leading to our picnic site formed a smooth, dry bridge manageable by any kindergartner. "What's the problem? Just jump across."

Brian and I were on a day hike with him, and I was feeling impatient and ready to get going. Sometimes it's morally righteous to push our kids to be brave, but sometimes it's merely pragmatic for the grownups around them. At other times it's important for me to honor Jack's fear. Common sense has helped me more than anything.

Even at six, the monkey bars were still too high and scary for Jack. But how much did that matter to me? At his friends' birthday parties, he still ordered me to go into the house with him and stay close by. But after ten minutes he would blush with embarrassment that I was still there, and tell me to leave. Boy, don't we all have many sides!

He was the only kid in his class to cry on the first day of kindergarten, but the very next day he was raising his hand to answer questions. Now he goes on merry-go-rounds, slides, trains and pony rides, but he still has to inspect things carefully first, like a structural engineer. He's one of the most "normal" people I know, yet he may never be one to "jump right in there and do it."

"I was *not* afraid of the merry-go-round!" Jack stomped into my room to protest while I was packing his bag for baseball practice. "You said it on the phone! You told Joan I was!"

"Don't you ever be ashamed to say you're afraid," I told him calmly, handing him his cap. "It's the most natural thing in the world. It can mean you're smart. Or you're sensitive.

"If you're too afraid to do something, you should never be blamed for not doing it! Or maybe you just don't want to do it badly enough. You'll do it when you're dang good and ready! I even think it would be great if someday you felt confident enough to express your fear to your friends, too, like you did with Daddy and me last weekend.

"You know, you could say, 'Have a good time hunting for snakes under the abandoned shed, guys! But me? No way! I'll be on that rock eating my peanut butter sandwich.' That would *really* show how brave you were!"

He just stared at me. I suddenly remembered, with some chagrin, that he *does* talk to his buddies this way. Even when he's blushing beet red, he's still been able to express his fear to his friends as well as to his parents—sometimes with tears, more often by putting it into words: "No, mom. It's too scary."

But at this stage, maybe it's more difficult for him *not* to say how he feels. The disguises just aren't in place yet. Maybe they don't ever have to be. If I can respect his fears, perhaps I can respect my own and stand up for both of us. I understand now how so much of this has been about me.

THE ENCHANTMENT

(or How to Start Your Own One-Woman Cult)

in which Joan paves a road with good intentions...

When it came to gurus with exclusive access to The Truth, I was as suspicious as the next person. In fact, I was suspicious *of* the next person. Still, I like to know which mind-controlling plot I'm fleeing before I join forces against it.

Imagine my chagrin, when whirling around to face the latest advancing horde of fanatics, I let out—not a scream of terror—but the asthmatic wheezing of guilty recognition: *Oh, my god! I'm One of Them!*

As an armchair crusader against brainwashing cults ever since one of them took an old friend, my sudden plunge into a Byzantine New Age Evangelical Spiritualism was undoubtedly perplexing to my small circle. Had I not been so busy my reforming my soul I might have enjoyed the irony.

One Christmas vacation, Linda and I got together with Mary at her house in Moraga. We laughed about being The City Mouse, The Country Mouse and The Suburban Mouse while our four children got to know each other.

The last time all three of us had been together was five years ago as the opening act in my *Yid Meets Shicksa* wedding reception. But something was different now. Not Linda. Or Mary. They seemed so comfortably familiar. And it wasn't the children. Maybe it was the fact that every sentence out of my mouth began with *"Rudolf Steiner says."*

Mary listened politely. As a human resources director, she'd probably heard it all. But I could see Linda was lonesome for the old Joan, now buried under a pile of dogma. Tell people how to correct their children's behavior, you will not be invited back. Tell them how to "enliven their soul forces" and you may find a deprogrammer at your door. I was lucky they put up with me till I exhumed myself.

I had never been a joiner of any kind, but something came over me when I read my first book about Waldorf education written by its creator, the spiritual scientist and philosopher, Rudolf Steiner. It was as if I were peeking through a keyhole into a mystical kingdom that was the secret inner life of childhood.

Steiner's passionate concern with nurturing and protecting the natural unfolding of the child's soul life awakened in me a deep feeling of reverence. At the heart of it all was the ancient principle that every aspect of education be imbued with *truth, beauty and goodness.* What a chord that struck within me! I was swept away!

It all began a year before the divorce. As a level-headed Jewish nerd, Thom was skeptical of the exacting Germanic nature of my latest eccentricity. But he did his best to humor me.

He even acted as begrudging accomplice in my plans for media elimination. No orthodox Waldorf home had a TV, so we were taking care of that.

"Isn't this a little extreme?" he asked between grunts. *Extreme?* How could anything so critical to the welfare of our child be *extreme?* I just gave him my *now-Thom-really-when-did-I-last-do-anything-in-moderation* laugh, and we lugged the Sony Soul-Stealer into the guest bedroom.

It would take some getting used to. Not for Graham, who couldn't sit still long enough to watch much of anything. But for me it would mean giving up my last pathetic connection to the world of film: my bedtime sci-fi movie.

Every night I picked out an old favorite and let its comforting clichés lull me to sleep. But I was ready to tough it out because I felt there was good reason to keep Graham away from the negative influences of media.

A fundamental maxim of Waldorf education advised that nothing be put before the child that was not worthy of his wholehearted unquestioning imitation. What a beautiful formula!

Evidently, inappropriate sensory input could harm the body as well as the mind. In their unfinished state of development the internal organs were susceptible to damage that might go unnoticed for awhile, but could later emerge as a crippling illness in adulthood.

Well, no problem there. I would just eliminate everything undesirable. That couldn't be too hard!

But I discovered to my horror, that according to Dr. Steiner, negative sensory input included harsh words, criticism and—oh my god—losing one's temper!

I had always felt guilty when I yelled at Graham, but now I found myself roasting on the spit of self-condemnation. How fast could I become spiritual? My son was almost four already—there was no time to lose!

I threw out all the plastic and bought wooden toys. I hung pictures of archangels and gnomes on every wall in Graham's room, and softened the corners with flowing arcs of pastel gauze. Thom's sarcastic, "It looks like a shrine in here," filled me with pride. I was on the right track. Soon I had a prayer ready for every meal, task, season, nature spirit, celestial being and mood swing. It was a regimen that made Islam look laidback.

One night Thom caught me sneaking out to dump a massive pile of videos into the garbage. He came down the front steps and we looked at each other in the moonlight, as motionless as deer and hunter.

Cautiously, he eased up to me as if I might be rabid. He didn't speak, just studied my face for any glimmer of sanity, and then wrestled a stack of tapes from my arms.

Undaunted, I pressed on in my crusade to purify everything. I was determined to build a protective sheath around Graham's childhood and swaddle him in the warmth and guidance of spiritual forces, even if those forces were beyond my comprehension.

I lived and breathed Rudolf Steiner, taking his ideas to heart. They all fit in with the plans I had for starting a nursery school. When I became single again, it was time to go into business.

I went beyond Graham's room to spread fairy dust in every corner of the house, until it was a rosy gossamer wonderland overflowing with natural and archetypal playthings—a veritable garden of truth, beauty and goodness!

Eventually there were four youngsters enrolled. My dream of a school of my own was coming true!

The children baked bread, molded beeswax and painted with organic plant-based watercolors. We played in a ring as cobblers or millers. We danced to songs of sunbeams and rainbows. Then, gathered round the puppet theatre, they would sit spellbound, watching a silken marionette weep in a cellar of straw or tumble down an enchanted well. As I did my best to bring those tales to life with simplicity and joy, I could almost feel myself becoming Amish!

Over the next two years my morning program grew into all day, every day childcare—with twelve children coming and going at all hours. It was a challenge to meet their divergent needs, and the non-stop company was hard on Graham, but I clung to Steiner's inspiration and added on more crafts, more story times, more hot steaming piles of spiritual sustenance.

As long as I kept plenty of activities going, everything was fine. Bubble-blowing over here, puppet-making over there, candle-dipping on the porch, third-shift lunch in the kitchen, and for the toddler who would eat no other way—applesauce-lapping from a bowl on the floor "like the dog."

I sang as I worked to keep my spirits up. These were delicate petals of life that opened out around me, and I'd read that my wellspring of negative thoughts could penetrate their ether bodies like ink on a blotter.

But by four o'clock I would find myself guzzling coffee and staggering. My speech was slurred and I always seemed to have one foot without a shoe on it. I managed to maintain a façade of competence until the children were picked up. Then it would hit. Implosion.

It was as if when the clock struck six, the spell wore off. Poof! My fancy ball gown of warmth and sensitivity was gone. In its place were the wretched rags of a depleted hag. Then the growling and grumbling would begin, and Graham would do his best to avoid me.

It was all I could do to get his dinner without blaming him for being hungry. Inevitably I would holler at him. After all my efforts throughout the day to protect and nourish his developing soul, there I was—crippling his little kidneys or spleen! But what was the distant future of a spleen compared to that all-too-immediate fear in his eyes?

In order to keep from frightening him any further, I would sprawl across the bed, turn on the VCR and intoxicate myself with some adrenaline-pumping, hostage-taking, car-exploding movie. And there Graham would be at my side, wide-eyed, enjoying the van Damm mayhem right along with me, soaking up images entirely unworthy of his unquestioning imitation!

But for that little while I could sit next to my son in a dumb-witted haze of tranquility. Through the flame-throwing and grenade volleys we sank into each other, comfortable and relaxed. I didn't even have the strength to beat myself up for exposing him to such stupidity.

So I couldn't be the fairy godmother after a twelve-hour day! At least there was a kickboxing action hero who could subdue the evil stepmother I'd turned into! The self-brain-washing was slowly losing its grip on me.

After another mind-numbing movie one night, we slid under the covers and I picked up *Wind in the Willows*, which we were reading again for the fourth time. I started in where we'd left off the night before. The automobile-obsessed Toad had just tricked Mole into fetching a lawyer so he could sneak out for a joy ride.

This was a time I treasured, when I could finally be myself. Curled up with my little boy in the crickety quiet of the night.

Graham was not a hugger. He didn't like any physical affection. But while I read to him he forgave my occasional pats or squeezes. I kept my rapture to myself as I admired the contours of his face, swooned in the smell of his hair or thrilled to the sublime heft of his legs as he plopped them across my own. I got away with adoring him.

I decided I wanted to go on adoring him and never frighten him again. I was sick of feeling guilty every night, and Graham deserved more than the leftover-Mommy scraps he was getting. What perverted sense of duty was driving me to continue in this cycle of torment? As I read about poor imprisoned Mr. Toad bemoaning his foolishness, I knew how he felt.

Although a pompous aristocrat, Toad's only way out was to disguise himself as a lowly washerwoman. He found it humbling and distasteful, but the choice was clear: he could remain incarcerated as a nobleman or go free as a peasant.

Maybe, like Toad, humility would be my salvation. It was time to give up my own inflated self-delusion of omnipotence. Stop pretending I could meet everyone's needs—or even wanted to. Graham's needs were challenge enough. It was time to close the daycare and admit defeat. It would be a small price to pay for taking the fear out of my son's eyes.

Had I really imagined myself capable of being an angelic presence to a dozen children seven days a week? Or even one small boy?

That Maternal Perfection Suit I'd been trying to squeeze myself into had become an iron maiden. It was never going to fit me, despite all the psychological liposuction I'd undergone to carve away all those *not-Waldorf-enough* parts of myself. But was a fairy godmother really necessary to my son's spiritual well-being? Or had that been *my* obsession? Now with my old nonconforming brain back, it seemed obvious that if Graham could have a plain old ordinary mother who cherished him, that would be good and true and beautiful enough.

LATE BLOOMER

(or When an Actress Lands the Biggest Supporting Role of All)

in which Linda tries to wedge a dream into time left over...

At first there was no response. Then a satisfying screech of outrage shattered the silence. But it was only Joan's cockatiels, the back up singers for our annual phone conversations.

"A bookie?" Joan's voice was as low and intimate now as if she were a revival tent preacher. *Amen* shrieked the gospel choir in the cage. "Your father?"

I shifted the phone to my left ear and shuffled through photocopies of old *Chronicles, Tribunes* and *Examiners* as I summarized the headlines about the San Francisco bust in '51. "My father's name is in almost every column."

"Your father was in San Quentin? The father who was so worried you'd fall off the straight and narrow and make him ashamed?"

"That father." I hadn't heard Joan speak with such force-fulness in years. Finally she was getting in touch with some anger! My anger, yes. But anger, nonetheless.

"How'd you find out?" she asked, over a bird whistle of amazement.

"My cousin Dennis in Massachusetts. I hardly ever talk to him, but he just mentioned it in passing during one of our catch-up phone conversations. He was surprised that I didn't know." I heard Joan speaking in soft tones to somebody.

"She doesn't want you to call her a girl. Uh huh... I know she's a girl, you're right. But that doesn't mean you call her a girl if she tells you she doesn't like you calling her that. Thank you."

"Who are you talking to? I thought you closed the day-care."

"Oh, I did."

"But isn't that a—"

"Some of the babies just washed back up with the tide."

"So you're still—"

"A doormat? Oh yes. You know being a doormat is a highly underrated skill. It's actually a dying art."

"You sound a little resentful."

"No. I am very resentful."

"Maybe that's good."

"Oh, you always like turning something bad into something good."

"Well—"

"So maybe you can turn one of those *Chronicles* into a party hat!"

'Yeah, I think that's what I'm doing right now. You know what else my cousin told me? He says my grandmother ran a brothel up in Marysville. He used to visit her there."

"A brothel?"

"Please don't say, 'Oh, how colorful,'" I warned.

"Oh, it is!"

"I asked you not to say that."

"I didn't say it. You did. I just agreed with you. It's *too* colorful. I just. God, Your dad was always on you."

"He was so adamant about my living up to something that I wasn't—"

"—something *he* couldn't even be. Well what do you make of it all?" Joan immediately settled into attentive-detached-therapist mode. And then, without even a segue, abandoned it. "I am so pissed!" Joan's intensity scared me a little, even when it was on my behalf. "This pisses me off! I remember you even had to lie to him about being a waitress so he wouldn't be ashamed of you."

"I can't help thinking of my mother. Taking care of a baby while her husband's in prison. I just can't see her as the supportive, forgiving type. I bet she wasn't very thrilled having to deal with me."

"But she went on pretending, just like he did. God, no wonder you can't hide anything. You're sort of the natural outcome of an unnatural situation."

"Yeah," I laughed.

"That equal and opposite reaction thing."

I stopped laughing, "Oh. Yeah." It all felt raw again. "I'll see you about five tonight at your mom's," I changed the subject. "We can talk more."

"You know what you should do?

"What?'

"The potato ritual. Remember? Throw the potato?"

"Yeah, well. I don't know."

"Or maybe you should bury a potato. No, I guess it's too late for that."

"I'll be okay," I shouted over the parrot shrieking that seemed to echo my own cognitive dissonance. I figured she had no idea what I'd already been through over the past week. I was pretty much catharted out. I needed her support and appreciated her righteous indignation. But I also wanted to feel closer to her. I needed her to need me, too.

Now that she was done with her esoteric little school, and almost fed up with being the Best Samaritan in the neighborhood, maybe she was on her way back down to earth. Or at least close enough to it so I could reach her. Hopefully, she could even open up to me about the details of her divorce. But she seemed so cheery now about Thom and how he was "really coming through." Yeah, I could see how Thom was more ex-husband than husband material. But did she have to vote him into the Hall of Fame just because he'd started paying child support?

I had to remind myself that I wasn't dependent on Brian the way she was on Thom. Or like my mother had been on my father. Both Joan and my mother shared a sort of pathetic determination to make things look the way they wanted them to. I didn't like the idea of squeezing the Cubist painting of your life into a Thomas Kinkade just so you wouldn't have to deal with your disappointment. It gave me vertigo.

Joan's stubborn optimism about our joint ventures in video and film, as much as I appreciated it, had never been that much help to me because it had never rubbed off.

But I wanted that optimism now. I wanted it for as long as I could soak in it. And perhaps my own unfiltered reality show might inspire Joan to scrape the layer of sofa painting off her beautiful Hieronymus Bosch.

I hadn't been to the old Alamo house in a long time and I was looking forward to it. Joan's mom had always seemed like the penultimate mother. The Madame of The House of Unconditional Love. The cultured but unassuming Mrs. Bechtel was as unlike my own parents as was the flamboyant grand-mother I'd just discovered. I was looking forward to seeing Ma Bechtel almost as much as I was to spending time with Joan.

As I turned off the 680 freeway to head into the rolling golden hills of Alamo, I was noticing something—not different, but actually too familiar, as I got out of the car at the top of Sugarloaf Hill. I couldn't help comparing the image I had of Joan's country cottage in Dutch Flat to the little stucco house on the hill in Alamo where she'd grown up.

Take away the encroaching subdivisions and the two-lane

roads, and the Bechtel homestead looked a lot like those quaint postcards of Dutch Flat she'd sent me. No wonder she'd wound up in that odd little town!

Alamo had changed a lot since Joan's childhood. No longer a smattering of pig farms and family ranches, it was now one of the most prestigious addresses in Northern California. As we crossed the checkered patches of crab grass her family was perfectly content to call a lawn, I realized how shocked my status-conscious mother would have been by this blatant disregard for keeping up with the Joneses. She would have needed to fit in with the Alamo Hoi Polloi.

For my mother pretense was not frivolous. It was serious business. Like a secret agent, she passed for Gentile when necessary and probably covered up my father's Big House time with a Lucy Ricardo yarn about his visit to the Old Country to discover his roots.

Like many Jews of her generation, my mother' ability to blend in was a survival skill learned as an immigrant child in Oakland. A skill I would probably never have. As much as I longed to feel more "normal," as much as I was at odds with my differentness, I couldn't seem to do anything about it. I admired the Bechtels' status apathy, the anti-establishment values, Joan's history of flaunting taboos. Even the house itself with its very used furniture and walls badly in need of paint was a beacon of defiance to conformity. But this comfort with not fitting in was almost as foreign to me as my own family's penchant for guile.

Joan's mom greeted me with a one-handed hug at the door. She was holding out a tiny pat of butter on a saucer. Peggy seemed frail now, but her wit and smile were as bright as ever.

"I put on lipstick just for you!" she said with a kiss.

"That pink brings out your glow, Peggy," I answered. "Whatcha got there?" I pointed to her plate.

"Oh, I don't know what to do with it," she puzzled slowly,

half to herself. "Should I wrap it up and put it in the refrigerator?" The dining room table was heaped with the usual pile of newsletters from Amnesty International and The Southern Poverty Law Center. This kind old lady found a little money for every good cause, but couldn't waste a pat of butter. Did toxic self-sacrifice run in this family? I was about to suggest the trash can, when I saw Joan flicking her mom's insulin needle at me like a switchblade. "Don't get involved," she hissed.

Clutching her melting Depression Era conundrum, Peggy followed us into the living room, marveling over Jack with a sincerity that shocked me a little. It was the same unadulterated, authentic warmth Joan used to exude before her well had run dry.

That evening, Joan and I tramped down the hillside and she gave me a tour of all her old childhood hideaways.

Under the eucalyptus had been the gypsy camp with furniture made out of hay. Over there, the acacia where she baked mud pies—and ate them. And here was the poplar spinney that had inspired the eleven-year old's dream to spend adolescence living as a mute beast-girl wearing only an animal pelt and calling herself Canus. I could almost see the free-spirited little girl who'd grown up to be such a—well, slagheap of delayed gratification.

As we stopped at the seventeenth tree I began to wonder if memory lane included the pine forest down the hill. But as she began eulogizing "the most beautiful cottonwood" that once held the tree-house her father had built, she choked on her words. Here it comes, I thought—the naked divorce court truth. Then she bursts out with a sniveling confession about how guilty she feels because *she* can stay home with her child and *I can't.*

I had to laugh—gently—because for years I'd been feeling sorry for *her*, stuck out there in the woods all by herself, diverting every ounce of her creative passion into motherhood.

Maybe if she'd been able to throw clay pots all day while rocking a cradle with her foot, I would have been jealous. Even as a working City Mouse, I was at least able to eek out a bit of time to create. I knew I could never survive what looked to me like a martyred life. I was the lucky one!

But after I returned home, I wondered about the freedom I'd been bragging about. Yes, I enjoyed more time for self-indulgence than ninety percent of the world. But the uncomfortable feeling inflating inside me like a bile-filled balloon was one I recognized right away: resentment, the feeling I'd always found to be the most excruciating. Resentment toward my father. Toward my mother. And spreading.

It was like kryptonite in way. Weakening me with humiliation—the embarrassing resurgence of feelings I thought I'd resolved twenty years ago. Blaming one's parents might be developmentally appropriate for a nineteen-year old. But for a gal hitting fifty? That seemed just plain juvenile.

The next evening I came home from work, home from a job I'd come to hate. A job that was positively burning me out. I dragged myself into the apartment to find two-year old Jack on the floor surrounded by all his amazing creations.

He'd drawn expressive scribbles of all shapes and sizes on colored paper in crayons and pastels, built a sort of Frank Lloyd Wright block structure, and was in the middle of performing a puppet show from some grand idea slowly unfolding in his brain.

"He's having a good time," Brian said casually.

"Great!" I said, while my real thoughts were: I can't believe I'm working at this stupid job all day so Jack can stay home to explore, expand, use his creative imagination, express who he really is, while I—*oh, no, stop! I can't believe I'm thinking such selfish thoughts!*

"Mommy, look!" Jack cried out. "Look here!" He proceeded to rub it in—showing me everything he'd made—just so he could hear a few appreciative words from his adoring mother. "Wonderful!" I croaked with all the enthusiasm I could force out. "Look at that! Beautiful!" I really did mean it, but—I can remember the shame—he was doing exactly what I wanted to be doing, and I wasn't getting to do it!

Boy, how mature! But wouldn't I love someone to work all day and support me, so I could stay home and find my artistic highs, my voice, my creative center?

Jack seemed to be growing by leaps and bounds in self-expression, while I felt myself shriveling up in a lowly position at a video post-production facility. All day I'd have to listen to the staff drop names of big movie stars as they worked on their films and videos. And therein lay the rub.

Not so many years before I'd been an actress myself, performing in Bay Area and Los Angeles theatre and in independent films. One of my shows had a two year run. I even had a recurring role on "The Young and the Restless." Well, that was all over. Now I was just old and restless.

I often thought back longingly to the good old days when Joan and I'd had our own grand artistic designs—a screenplay, a production company, years full of ideas, and a comic timing together we couldn't believe ourselves. We were certain we were on the verge of *knockin' 'em dead*. Though never a movie star, I had once at least been on the bottom rung of show business. Now I was on the bottom rung of a clerical pool.

Just before my acting career started to fizzle out, I wrote a monologue, and found I enjoyed the writing more than the acting. From then on, writing was my new passion. I took classes and re-organized my life so I could write every day.

So there I was in my 40's, with a kid, an office job and a dream. A dream, I might add, that I took quite seriously. But since I hadn't been published, I couldn't really call it a career. And how I longed to call it that.

My mother always told me, "You can fall in love with a

rich man as easily as a poor one." I never succeeded. When I think of aspiring film actresses who somehow end up married to wealthy producers or financiers—allowing them to pursue their dreams and careers—I wonder how they pulled it off.

None of my past boyfriends ever focused much on making a lot of money or on supporting me so they could feel important or beneficent. They were all funny, creative guys. *What an idiot I've been.*

And then I went and married for love, with Brian being, in my mind of course, the cleverest, funniest and most creative of all. But definitely not rich. What's a gal gonna do?

My lack of time and energy was a trial, but it wasn't the source of my alienation. After reading one of those "have-it-all" articles about a mother struggling to juggle children and career, I'd ask myself, "So what career do *you* have? You're not even doing what you want to be doing yet!"

The pain of that realization has sometimes made me want to lie in bed for a few days with the covers pulled tightly over my head. What about those of us juggling children, a day job, and a *dream?* Especially when we're not so young anymore!

I've often wondered. Is it really so bad to be older and still trying, trying, trying? When I'm honest with myself, I don't think so at all.

I find it interesting and inspiring to see so many people over forty-five turning to new careers or trying to establish themselves in new ways. I'm glad Jack has been exposed to the idea that even with obstacles—getting older, lacking time and money, overdosing on self-doubt—a person (like his mother, for example) can keep on plugging ahead. I reveled in the realization that he was growing up with such different expectations than I had.

The tragedy of my family's dark side was not how they'd made money. Bookmaking and brothels. Why would I care? It was the shame they took on, that legacy of denial. If only my father had been able to take pride in being a bookie, *a big macher*! And my grandmother valued as a free-spirited entrepreneur! It was the exhausting work of repression that I think hurt us all the most.

I had never managed to repress much of anything. I started wondering if Jack might actually benefit from this oddball characteristic of mine. His growing up without family secrets certainly wouldn't hurt.

One morning Jack lay on my bed working on his art, doing a self-portrait, while I sat at the computer pounding out my second novel. I turned around and caught him glowing from having discovered some new stroke of the crayon. I felt suddenly lucky to be able to witness so often such heightened, unadulterated human curiosity and creativity. It was inspiring to be able to watch Jack constantly dream.

But I still felt jealous of him. He didn't know about feelings of failure. He didn't need to take time away from his artistic endeavors to work a day job. He didn't have his ego wrapped up with what he was creating.

Of course I would always want to support him emotionally, so that his life could be as rich and full as possible. Not just in childhood, but as an adult, too. For his sake—as well as mine—I had to resist the temptation to call myself a loser because I hadn't made my own dreams a reality. Maybe my example could help him understand that growing up didn't mean giving up.

I'm a lot older than Jack, but my creative impulse, drive and ability are still going strong. We're in this together. We're both still discovering, and if I'm lucky, that will never end.

HIS OLD ALMA MARTYR

(or Lesson Plans of Shame)

in which the gods die and leave Joan in charge...

My mother always said, "It takes all kinds to make a world." I knew that meant be tolerant of others. But looking back at all the support, understanding and unconditional love she gave to me—her wildest child, I realize now that the "all kinds" I was supposed to be tolerant of—included me!

Linda never got that same kind of encouragement for her creativity. But maybe that's why she became such an impassioned advocate of self-expression. For her, the ancient edict, *Know thyself*, was only one part of the equation. *Be thyself* was just as important. For Linda it wasn't just a handy axiom, it bordered on pathological condition.

Her inability to *not* be herself was her Achilles' heel. But it was also what helped people like me to accept their darker feelings. That was what I learned from Linda—and forgot, and had to learn again, over and over through the years of our friendship.

This faith in self-acceptance and self-expression even affected our parenting decisions in similar ways—like education. We wanted our kids to be in a place where they could be themselves. Jack needed academic challenge. Graham needed less pressure. But they both needed to be accepted as they were.

When Linda first told me about the variety of great public school options in the Los Angeles area, I was more than a little jealous. How I missed the advantages of urban living! In a big city one size is not expected to fit all! There's room for different races, religions, politics, and the uncategorizably unorthodox. There was Linda—sitting in L.A.'s educational lap of luxury—with her two *(count'em two)* item list of Jack's educational needs: 1. lots of different kinds of kids, 2. enough money for field trips. And here I was, banished by Thom's corporate relocation to the back lot of this arid Aryan empire with a wish list longer than the state budget.

The foothills seemed to be the new Mecca for angry white males or "voluntary segregationists" as they preferred calling themselves, who'd fled the "ungodly miscegenation" of the mono-cultural Contra Costa County of my youth. They'd stuck it to the Shell Man and migrated upstream to explore the entrepreneurial opportunities of deer rendering and fast meth-lab chains.

Thom and I never got over the culture shock of Auburn, but we did our best to blend in. My liberal bumper stickers not only aroused enthusiastic finger thrustings on the road, at home in my crime-free neighborhood they ignited our next door neighbor's shooting spree and a SWAT team presence rivaling Waco. I quickly tried to denude the vehicles of all things "un-American." The Honda emblem wouldn't budge, but I managed to scrape off "Health Care for Everyone," "KPFA" and the cute evolved fish sticker that screamed: "PLANT CAR BOMB HERE."

I began to censor myself, carefully keeping *woman* and *equal* out of the same sentence. I was stuck here and I'd better try to fit in. I was learning to live without free speech, organic coffee and central heating, but I'd be damned if I wouldn't beat the bushes till I found some real educational options.

As soon as Graham was three, I began dragging him around the Sierra foothills to explore his future. After visiting more than twenty schools, I realized a student-directed education might not be available outside the Bay Area.

Like many parents, I was determined that my son would go to the best school. Not the most prestigious or the most exclusive. Not the one with the highest test scores. The best school for Graham would be the one that valued and trusted him the most. A Summerhillian sort of a program like my first son had attended, where children were encouraged to take responsibility for their own learning, progress at their own pace, and tie-dye their own shirts.

But when I began looking around, I wondered if the human potential movement had been run out o' them thar parts. Every school I visited seemed to operate, not according to Maslow's psychological theories of self-realization or Piaget's developmental studies, but closer to the warehousing wizardry of Sam *Walmart* Walton.

I finally found a beautiful school with an open-classroom, an art and dance studio, horses and a pool. With an enrollment of five it seemed ideal.

A few months later, however, I was notified that our imperfect attendance was not acceptable. "I have to come here every day whether I like it or not," his teacher flared. "How is he going to learn responsibility? How will he hold a job?" He was not yet four. Did he really need to worry about his resume?

"What are you going to do when he starts Kindergarten? You're not thinking of *homeschooling* him, are you?" she asked, as if such folly led straight to Satan's own recruiting office.

But really—*homeschool?*

Wasn't homeschooling only for armed compounds of inbred survivalists where great broods of children recited scripture till they keeled over in an oxygen-deprived dither of zeal for the Lord? Why would I want to do that?

Cloistered indoctrination was not my idea of education. My idea of education was broad and inclusive—well, except for *homeschooling*. I'd come down with pedagogophilia (morbid obsession with educational philosophy) in high school when I read A.S. Neill. Pedagogophiles—the opposite of Xenophobes—have only one fear, and that's The Anal Master of Uniformity. (I divorced him in '79, but he takes many forms.)

Pedagogophiles (and we make up a good .00002% of the population) have a deep and abiding terror of the body-snatching, mind-control of group think. For us, the pursuit of happiness, social justice and democracy itself depends on pluralism. So when I turned my life and my will over to Steiner as I understood him, Linda lost not just a friend, but maybe a little part of herself too. That part that didn't exist unless Joan reflected it. I had been absorbed into the Borg.

It happened not long after I pulled Graham out of that "perfect" school. My spiritual conversion. Transforming me from an annoying advocate of free schools into an annoying devotee of Rudolf Steiner.

My heart was full of joy when Graham was old enough to go to kindergarten at the local Waldorf school. I knew he would be nurtured there for the unique individual he was. His sensitivities would not be labeled defects to be cured, but cherished as mysteries that would later unfold to reveal more of who he was meant to be. Unfortunately, there were twenty-seven other children in his class—one of them a bully—whose mysteries were all equally cherished.

Every day after school, we used his little wooden dolls to re-enact the day's torments in order to patch up his emotional wounds. His angelic teachers reassured me this was not too much for Graham to handle. However, it became too much for me—having to overpower his wailing and kicking every morning to maneuver him into the car.

So after three months we dropped out of kindergarten. I felt like a failure. Maybe my lack of backbone had just cut my child off from what could have been the most valuable experience of his life. Maybe I couldn't teach him responsibility. Maybe he *would* grow up to be a hobo.

I had never fully trusted my parenting, but I had always trusted my children. When the first two dropped out of high school for a couple of years, I thought, Why not? Who wouldn't?

In junior college they sampled different majors and took time out to pursue careers in real estate and cosmetology. It seemed to me my job was to keep my opinions to myself, be supportive and stay out of the way. Eventually, after following the winding paths of their own interests, one became a psychiatric nurse, the other a surgeon.

But I wasn't so sure of myself anymore. Maybe Graham needed to be pressured or bribed or cajoled. Since I was unable to do any of those things, I would just have to forge a new path based on what I perceived to be Graham's needs. Even if we ended up two hobos on the Road to Ruin, at least we'd be whistling.

Like true drifters with no plans for the future we left the past behind—and came stumbling in through the back door of homeschooling. I'd always felt there was a perfect school out there for every child. Now I had to be it!

Teaching kindergarten with Waldorf methods was not too difficult. I'd studied early childhood education for three years in college, I'd been a nursery school teacher, and I'd designed my daycare around Steiner's approach. But the following year when it came time for formal instruction, I was terrified and remorseful.

I'd wanted my son to have that beautiful arts and nature focused integrated curriculum, resonating with spiritual truth. A pure and undiluted Waldorf education. But no, he wouldn't be dining on seven courses of psychic nourishment. He was getting a TV dinner—a starchy pedagogical pot pie of Rudolf Steiner, Joan Baez and Roger Corman.

I spent hours developing lessons that could be danced, moved, rhymed and sung, but usually they just fell flat. I tried to blame Graham.

"If you're too tired to cooperate, you can just go take a nap until you're ready for circle time!" That certainly snuffed out any flicker of spiritual inspiration still smoldering in the whole shebang.

Eventually I bent my self-imposed rules and followed Graham's lead, letting his curiosity and wonder guide us. After all, there was no rush.

That's one reason I'd moved to the rustic hinterland. So he could take his time growing up. He could wander the hills, hike down to the river, or straddle a log in the pond to catch tadpoles. It was a place he could have a Huck Finn childhood with freedom to explore and imagine.

Sometimes I would overhear him constructing one of his make-believe plays. "Now you pretend you didn't hear me coming. You only heard a big ol' owl hoot, but there was not supposed to be any hoot owls, so you look back and call me, but there's no reply. Then you notice the window's still open, and suddenly you hear a creak and you see a little bit of my rope coming out from under the door..." My heart would sing. This was what it was all about.

Yet, inevitably, the choice to homeschool attracted some unsolicited concern.

When Graham was about seven and a half, I had a visit from my neighbor. We talked while our kids played. Well, she talked. I listened. I knew better than to open myself up and offer criticism a martini.

I did grab some sodas and rice cakes for the kids, though. Grace handed a can to Graham and asked him to check the ingredients. When she saw the blank look on his face, she was aghast. "Isn't he reading yet?"

As I turned away to shoo Graham out of the kitchen and think of an answer, a sweet magnolia voice purred through my head. It was Chinette, exhaling a churning cloud of Lady Kent Menthol Light 100's. "Honey, he'll read just as soon as you hand him somethin' *worth* readin' like the swimsuit edition of *Guns and Ammo!*"

But I didn't have Chinette's Cracker charisma or possum-skinning nerve anymore. And I knew I couldn't fit into the Halter Top of Shamelessness. So I fretted.

Isn't he reading... was this a problem? Gosh, I'd been rather enjoying Graham's illiteracy.

I loved reading to him and telling him stories. He was singing and dancing, acting in little fairytale plays, and playing recorder. But nobody ever asked me, "Can he tour jete?" "Does he know any African brush-cutting songs?" or "How many knots can he tie in a string?" How I could have bent some-one's ear over those accomplishments!

I had actually been hoping that teaching him to read would be like an old time sea voyage—long and slow—so I could savor it. But the shocked tone of my neighbor's question made me wonder if she thought I was raising another Kaspar Hauser.

My mind raced. I could hear the hangin' judge banging his gavel.

All rise. Reading Rainbow Court is now in session.

I was new at this homeschooling thing. Was allowing a seven-year old to remain illiterate something I could be put in jail for? I'd known women who had lost custody of their chil-dren for less. Surely I could come up with some alibi for seven years without phonics.

Maybe it was time for some witness box histrionics to flush out the real criminal in the courtroom—"He made me do it! That's why my son can't read! I was too busy exploring his human potential because of—*that* man and his hoity-toity

Hierarchy of Needs! That's him—right there—Abraham Maslow!"

Or I could plead *non compos mentis.*

The witness will answer the question.

All right, let's see. What if I drew her a quick diagram of how oral storytelling multiplied neuropathways in the brain? Or maybe I could demonstrate some of the exercises I use to coordinate smooth bilateral functioning. How about summarizing the results of that longitudinal study linking accelerated academics to depression?

The witness will please—

Maybe I could take the jury hostage, "I've got a flimsy excuse—don't make me use it!" No. I knew when I was beaten. I turned back to the prosecutor sitting at my kitchen table, still holding out an unopened Exhibit A.

My face a mask of contrition, I pled my case. "He's getting there," I stammered. Defense rests.

But he *was* getting there! And that was the main reason I was homeschooling Graham. So he could get there—wherever "there" happened to be—in his own time and in his own way. It was what happened in between "here" and "there," what treasures we unearthed along the way that mattered to me the most.

No, he wasn't an academic powerhouse at age seven. Couldn't College Bowl wait?

Graham's real prowess was in the area of social skills. At age eight, his powers of friendly conflict resolution dwarfed those of some teenagers I knew. Graham even shocked me sometimes. "Tell me, Mom," he would say, "what feelings are locked up inside you?"

But apparently facts are not as powerful as beliefs. Over and over again—with my little psychological savant right there at my side—I heard it. *The* Question. The mother of all homeschooling FAQ's: "How will he learn social skills? Aren't you isolating him too much?" The tone is urgent, suspicious—yet seeking no answer, like a one-minute McCarthy hearing.

Well, I suppose I had found that close-knit community I'd been wishing for ever since I left Palo Alto—I just hadn't expected the spilling over of lives to bury me in a mudslide. What ever happened to the gentle art of shunning?

Maybe this shock and disapproval sprang from the gospel of compulsory education that sanctioned The School as lone inculcator of social norms. But did teachers even want that job?

I mean, how much civilizing could you really do with teacher-student ratios of one-to-twenty inside and one-to-a hundred outside? It seemed to me I had a better shot at it with my one-on-one.

More likely the isolation question was a thinly veiled accusation that I was some kind of paranoid anti-government extremist. Well, sure, maybe I was a little bit driven by a fear-fueled determination to defend my child against every real or imagined emotional, social, physical or supernatural danger. But that did not make me one of those raving xenophobes! On the other hand, they really didn't seem all that irrational anymore.

Despite my overzealous supervision, Graham enjoyed a healthy social life. As a childcare provider I had plenty of opportunity to model social skills that Graham could practice in real life situations.

But after I closed the daycare things changed. The playmate population dwindled. Over the next two months, three of Graham's closest friends moved away. Our little mountain village just seemed to keep shrinking.

We took advantage of our time alone together. We went swimming and hiking, played tennis, basketball and endless hours of chess. But he missed his friends, and I was tormented by guilt for homeschooling him into a corner.

I tried to reassure myself that in other places and other times children had overcome the challenges of loneliness. During the Westward expansion. On the tundra. In times of plague. I knew I needed to have faith that this period of scarcity would end. Naturally I forgot that that kids in school can also experience loneliness. I just assumed our homeschooling was the cause, and re-evaluated that choice on a daily (or even hourly) basis.

I finally came to him, completely defeated. "You need friends. I think we need to put you in school so you can be with friends." He threw his arms around me—something he never did. "No!" he insisted. "I love my homeschooling!"

His blithe acceptance of that bleak world only ignited my primal urge to bag a small child and bring it home for him.

Actually there were dozens of homeschoolers in our community. The problem was—they were archconservative fundamentalists—the nemesis of liberals, Jews, Muslims, gays, anyone who spoke English as a second language and all the rest of The Lord's children who'd disappointed Him in some way. The worshippers of a Tough Love God: "Believe me, sending you to Hell hurts me more than it does you!" And look out! I seemed to be walking around with a scarlet "A" on my forehead. Not for *adultery*, but for all those really awful "A" words like *atheism, affirmative action* and *AFDC*. But surely it was possible these parents no more fit my paranoid stereotype of "insensitive right-wingers," than I fit theirs of a "radical libber."

Nobody's inherently cruel! If we scapegoat, it's out of fear, isn't it? And fear is an autocrat. Not a parliament. I'd learned that when clinical depression had put my own threat perception center in charge of processing all brain activity. But if these were fear-ruled people, they seemed anything but depressed. In fact, they never seemed to have any conflict whatsoever. Maybe their inner Homeland Security had a little more to it than mine had.

To my Orwellian way of thinking, the Fundamentalist monitored her long twisting line of foreign ideas and insurgent feelings with more than a metal detector. I pictured Gestapos whisking off undesirable thoughts to internment camps and cattle cars. With enough cranial redirection and warehousing, that snaking line of incoming stimuli would never bog down: *You—in the ecology getup—to Displacement! You with the Darwin theory—over there with the scapegoats. You! Yeah, you flaunting your damn Relativism—get in line for the stoning.*

For my son's sake, I would have to put aside my paranoid prejudices and summon the courage to cross enemy lines. But it would take more than an apple pie and an open mind to break through that Fundamentalist Wall. Unless... Unless I could make myself less threatening. Then came divine inspiration—how to swing a rope bridge between Sodom and Salem.

I found an old worm-eaten Bible. Well, when in Rome, use Vatican bait! At the top of the pile of books I schlepped every day to the park I placed what appeared to be Dutch Flat's most obsessively consulted copy of the Good News. And eventually it worked. They came out of the woodwork. Children my son's age.

Naturally, there was the obligatory "Do you love Jesus" test administered by a solicitous six-year-old girl. My attempt to sidestep with a warm, "I think everybody does in their own way, don't you?" was vehemently rebuffed. "Oh, no! They follow Satan and do everything he says!" I hastily nodded agreement and her anxiety rushed out in a rapturous sigh. Now I was welcomed as sort of an auxiliary Junior Baptist on probation.

As I spent more time among the Righteous, it became obvious these parents weren't monsters. They were friendly, kind—even intelligent and compassionate. I liked them. In fact, I admired them. And I felt a little ashamed of my charade.

Still, even though I was accepting occasional invitations to services and potlucks, I knew I wasn't fooling anybody, so I braced myself for the inevitable burning cross in my yard. (After all, Nazi Germany had been full of nice people.) But the mob never showed. And although Graham was expected to get down on bended knee and pray for God's forgiveness whenever he used the word *Dang*, he didn't seem to mind. It was an escape clause. How else could those godly children sleep at night knowing their buddy was doomed to eternal Hell fire? To Graham, the genuflection was simply a chore like brushing his teeth. I still worried he would wake up some night screaming about being left behind with sea-sucking angels. But he never did.

As anti-ERA, -EPA, and -ACLU as they may have been, on one level I fit right in. In this subculture homeschooling was *de rigueur*. Unlike my overly friendly neighbors, these folks didn't spy on me with binoculars or tell my son he was "abnormal." As a single, Unitarian mom in the Village of The Saved, I suddenly found myself on the same side as my own worst nightmare. It was an acceptance I never experienced in the more liberal world I'd always called kin.

Family, friends, even clerks at the DMV seemed to feel an obligation to rescue me from the folly of home education. Some lectured. Some begged us to "give school a chance." But why this *noblesse oblige* to civilize the savage homeschooler?

My first interrogation had taken place—appropriately enough—in front of the old historic Dutch Flat schoolhouse. Graham and I were just leaving the tennis court at the park next door.

"Beautiful, isn't it!" said a tourist about my age with a camera around her neck, smiling up at the bell tower.

"Oh, yes." I agreed.

"So, no school today?"

I put on my Alfred E. Neumann grin. "We're homeschoolers."

"Ohhhhh," she said in that all too familiar *surely-you-know-better-than-that* tone. I hoped she would assume I was a fundamentalist and dismiss my parental stupidity as religious fanaticism. But no. Apparently she could see right into my under-zealous Unitarian heart.

She crossed her arms and cocked her head. "How will he learn socialization?" My first impulse was to blurt out," *The real question is, Madam—when will you?"* But I held my tongue. In a tiny village like mine unpleasant words did not dissolve into the mix of competing histories as they did in the city. They became indelibly inscribed on a sort of piss-ant Akashic Record, resounding through the generations. From the hobo fires of The Diggin's to the militia camps on Moody Ridge and right on back to this very monument to provincial authority, the one–room schoolhouse. It was an oral tradition passed down with extreme prejudice.

Her eyebrows arched, my Grand Inquistitrix allowed the customary five seconds for me to repent. It was *Final Jeopardy.*

I suppose she imagined the question had never occurred to me before. *Hmmm... socialization...Hey, thanks! I guess I should look into that!* But come on, Graham learned social skills from his parents like all children did. *See?*—I wanted to point out to her—*Notice how he's not kneeing you in the groin right now? That's because I'm showing him we don't knee smug milksops in the groin, no matter how much they deserve it.*

But that question—How *will* he learn socialization... it sounded like I hadn't even started yet. All the years I'd put into helping him learn to talk about feelings, laugh at jokes that aren't funny, duck and cover when mommy goes off—and it didn't show? I couldn't help wondering if where I saw a normal third-grader, she saw Ishi, Last of His Tribe.

"It's hard in a small town," I giggled submissively over my

shoulder. I practically leaped up the hill to the street, nearly yanking Graham's arm out of its socket.

I'd never felt the urge to don robes (well—*bathrobe,* actually—arcane symbol of the homeschooling mom) and recruit converts at the airport. So why all the fuss to deprogram *me?* What did I represent that made people roll their eyes, forecast cultural devolution, and suddenly remember colonoscopy appointments?

Who was I threatening? The teacher's union? The backpack industry? Or was it something more nebulous?

The hostile reactions to *H-The Unschooled* were probably triggered by some dark dread buried deep in the collective psyche. *"They're here! Usurpers From Beyond the Norm! Grab your status quo and get out!"*

What was there about the socialization of a homeschooler that stirred up such a hornet's nest of cultural angst? Did it smack of *too much* Americanism—nationalistic and ethnocentric? Or *not enough*—too anarchistic maybe? Gosh, it could be that what I was doing in my crumbling cottage—right there between the blackboard and the kitchen table—was un-American. Perhaps, like a pedagogically perverted Dr. Moreau, I was creating from my gory philosophical patch-work—not a social being, but an abominable beast-man, both social scourge and jungle Pariah. I'd probably been brainwashed back during the Human Potential Movement!

Yes, it was their fault! Crackpot agitators like A.S. Neill, John Holt and Soupy Sales should really be brought up before a House Subcommittee on UnAmerican Socialization Activities.

But an ounce of prevention is worth a pound of punishment. Forget socialized medicine. We need medical socialization!

No high end laser gismos. Just a one-step, out-patient adjustment on Big Brother's *Dis*-assembly-line, requiring only a brief encounter with a standard hydraulic apple-coring device.

Cheap, quick, sanitary! But even a Leni Riefenstahl would have a tough time hyping lobotomy and castration as the latest stress-reducing *must-have's* in social-surgery. So, until then, how do we "get socialized?"

How do we make human beings out of the little seeds of human potential sheathed in animal urges? I used to think it was simple.

You take a human being. *(the child)*
Add society. *(the family)*
And toss. Voila!

You can add whatever else you want, but a salad is still mainly just lettuce and dressing. Yet people were turning up their noses at mine. It was missing some secret ingredient.

Obviously, socialization had something to do with character and citizenship. Didn't it? But even those concepts mean one thing to a Quaker and another to a Navaho. In fact, socialization might be one of those subjective things like art—*I don't claim to understand socialization, but I know what turns my stomach.*

The Big Socialization Issue was probably not really a controversy over manners and social skills *per se.* Maybe it was more about the democratic ideal of uniting a diverse people under a common set of values. As The Fairly Adequate Equalizer, school did exert its mitigating influence—broadening the narrow-minded and reigning in the wackos. A sort of benign Procrustean bed.

I wondered if Linda thought I was keeping my child out of the melting pot for some elitist reason. Putting our children in mixed race schools had been important to both of us. Unfortunately, up where I now lived there was only one race. But was that really the only way to produce a sensitive, cooperative, socially aware and culturally-open child fit for democracy? Doesn't life itself round off our sharp corners, widen our horizons, and lop off our inflated egotism? Yes—Life does.

But maybe not in the most organized, uniform and predictable way.

Maybe what was taught in the classroom was perhaps less important than the organizational structure itself—the medium being the message—as Marshall McLuhan might say. With protocol to follow, standards to achieve and deadlines to meet, children can practice on the bunny slopes of the Puritan work ethic. Lacking this, would my child be unprepared for employer expectations of productivity, time management, and not passing notes to your neighbor about the union meeting? I could barely get him to brush his teeth.

But perhaps I was, like the blind men and the elephant, grabbing at the wrong end of the beast. Maybe the schoolroom wasn't the real sphere of influence. Maybe what mattered was what went on just outside.

For generations the schoolyard has been glorified as *The One True Socializer.* One friend thought Graham should go to school so he could "learn to fight like a man." Even as bully containment policies and student mediator programs were becoming more common, there seemed to be a not-in-my-backyard resistance to it in my neck of the woods. Perhaps out of reverence for the old days when sacking villages was *in.*

But what is the mystique that immortalizes this legendary vortex of peer power? Perhaps, as modern mystery center for trials by torment, the blacktop jungle provides a microcosm for the grown-up world of juntas, HMO's, and custody battles. Maybe bullies and cliques offer the equivalent of poisonous snakes and desert thirst in a Western version of the Aboriginal Walkabout. But actually, if being called "Pecker Brain" at recess built character, I was pretty sure I could replicate that at home.

Contrary to popular folklore, however, homeschoolers are not exempt from these vital social experiences. When school's out, tyrants find other places to cull the weak from the herd, like the neighborhood park.

That's where my child, along with all the others, got to flex his Lizard Brain in personal growth encounters with apes evolved from men. The only difference was—I was there with him, a meddling missionary camouflaged as a catalog-browsing hausfrau, but ready to spring at a moment's notice into Day Of Reckoning conflict-resolution assault action. Yes, they all mocked me! Our little park was safe and secure and didn't need *no newcomer buttinskis.* But like the steadfast Don Quixote, I remained undaunted in my delusional crusade.

Wherever there was a kid lynching another kid's kitten, whenever there was a bully flinging a geek, wherever there was a hothead carving a popsicle stick into a shiv, I was there, talking him down, negotiating the hostage release, praising anything resembling an I-message. Until that day She showed up.

Confederate Flag Barbie. Fixin' for a showdown at the monkey bars. She wants a *piece o' me* for dragging her boy into "talking about feelings" one too many times. "My mom's gonna whup you!" snickers her sidekick. Normally I eschew the quaint local custom of extemporaneous Claim-Jumping Re-enactments. But now the last three years of torment descend upon me in a seedy film noir montage. The huge distorted faces crowd in: "HOW WILL HE LEARN SOCIALIZATION? *Zation ... zation... zation...* ISN'T HE READING? *Reading.... reading... reading...* FIGHT LIKE A MAN! *Like a man... a man... a man...* Well, okay! Bring it on!

Slowly I rise. An angry breeze whips my flowered hippie skirt across my legs. The sunset ignites my red head into a blazing Shiva. The lonesome whistle of a desperado Western sounds my vengeance. I am one bad mother! Time stops for the moment of truth. And when I open my eyes—she's giving her hot pants a *so-what, yer not worth it* tug, and turning away to prance home, wincing, across hot rocks in bare feet. What did it? My shining resolve? My higher purpose? The hundred pounds I had on her?

In the end I had my reward: a kid who could play at the park to his heart's content without suffering lifelong trauma, a kid who could negotiate his way through almost anything, a kid who kept his faith in humanity by learning to run like the devil.

I would never be able to convince anyone that children could grow up well-socialized without schools. Not even Linda. Because she so carefully avoided the subject, I knew she was protecting me from her disapproval. Luckily, selling anyone on the idea wasn't my job. All I had to do was convince myself that it was okay to trust the choice I'd made for my own child.

But many of us—whether stay-at-home or working, private, home- or public-schooler, Christian or Muslim—wear a sign that says, "Correct my parenting, please!" I learned to keep my homeschooling aberration below radar. And if I was caught—just smile sweetly. "Gosh, thank you! And all this time I thought that little rascal was going to school! I'll fix his wagon!"

For me, homeschooling meant fewer things to regulate, demand and correct. It gave us the freedom to wander, rather than race. To learn about life, rather than worry about getting socialized. True blessings for an irresponsible taskmaster like me.

Sometimes in the middle of a story I was telling Graham, I would stop—not sure what was going to happen next. It was a pause filled with wonder and expectancy. As if we were adrift between two chords in a melody, enjoying the fading resonance of the first, anticipating the pathos of the next—floating in the interval that would make them into music. This was how I felt about being a part of Graham's education.

It was a journey of discovery that would take us to many new lands. But we'd have to navigate past the Hidden Reef of

Resentment, through the towering swells of my overindulgence, and around the Swirling Vortex of Guilt. Yet every expedition had its perils. And Graham would survive his. After all, this was his story and he was the hero. How he conquered, endured or adapted to the challenges of bullies, Bible-thumpers, a visiting dad, an omnipresent mom—all of these would shape his legend. He was the captain of his fate. And in the end, it would be his tale to tell.

I would have to wait and see. For now, I had to allow a person to take his own shape from our little mudball of shared humanity. From our ideals and our mistakes. The petty squabbles and the questions too big to answer.

As I watched this messy sculpting-from-the-inside wobble out into the world I knew there was hope—for all the children who couldn't do it the way everybody else did. For every parent worried that his child wouldn't fit in. For all the unsung heretics who've resisted the siren call of normality, guarding pluralism against the Individuality-snatchers and Dark Lords of Uniformity.

In my sagging cottage as old as the pledge of allegiance, where floorboards ripple gently in amber waves of grain, right here in our own humble cradle of civilization between the blackboard and the kitchen table, we'll be reading *Homer Price*, practicing cursive, and keeping democracy safe.

BARBIE AND BATMAN
DUEL TO THE DEATH

(or a Case of Nature vs. Nurture)

in which Linda pleads, "No Opinion, Your Honor..."

I never realized Joan suspected I disapproved. I was always very careful in our conversations about homeschooling. I tried to keep an open mind. In fact, it was years before I realized I had been a little judgmental in the beginning. Out of fear I suppose. I thought she'd turn into on of those paramilitary mamas. At least our differences never came to a head. We never went *hermana a hermana* in a smackdown over ideology. Probably because she had one and I didn't. Besides, we both had too many individual battles to fight when it came to motherhood and the societal and personal *shoulds* that plagued us.

Joan felt pressured to mother less, I to mother more. It was often difficult for us to understand each other's polar opposite enigmas. Yet at a deeper level we were probably facing the same conflict: How do we reconcile who we really are with who we feel we're supposed to be? What we really needed from each other was what we'd always counted on in our friendship: trust. Trust that every human being knows best how to solve her own problems. Not so easy when you have to stand by and watch your best friend go over to the dark side.

The image of Joan as a homeschooling mother didn't make much sense to me. Chinette in her peek-a-boo bustier, teach-

ing sex education from a *Hustler* to her six-year old—that I
could picture. But what about Joan—especially the new spiri-
tually-correct Joan? Could she really squeeze herself into the
pinched-up persona of a one-room school marm? If she could,
I wasn't sure I'd want to watch. But the whole concept of
homeschooling just didn't make sense to me.

I'd always felt Joan and I were working in the same paradigm on the same social agenda. Trying to do our insignificant
bit to make the world a little more tolerant. And here she was
separating her child out from the rest of creation. I felt
betrayed. What a turncoat! Could she really be serious about
this plot against her own life?

Yes, apparently she could. And she was working awfully
hard at it! Like John Henry against the machine. I had to
admit—I was a more than a little intimidated. If Joan was willing to give up her entire existence for this *fahrshtunkener*
homeschooling, she must think I'm a completely uncaring,
irresponsible excuse for a mother to ship my kid off to public
school. Well, I'd show that *chutzpadik!* I'd just keep right on
sending my son to public school!

But over the years, my discomfort eased as Joan told me
about how it worked for Graham. She'd never believed homeschooling was right for all kids. All she knew was that it seemed
to be the natural choice for Graham. But what about Joan's
needs (if she even noticed them anymore)? That was the part
that didn't fit. I just couldn't imagine her choosing to homeschool of her own volition.

"Let's see now—should I make another art film? Or—
start a girl's group? Hey, how about I throw my personal life
in the stump grinder and homeschool my son for twelve years?
Sure!" But Joan had long been a crusader for radical school
reform. I could see how homeschooling might be satisfying
her urge to bring down The Man

Although I had strong feelings about social justice myself,

they were tamer. I was never much of an activist, unless you include drinking and dancing at AIDS benefits. Joan, however, put the *free* in free speech.

She accosted shoppers with petitions, unleashed Chinette at fundraisers, and whether it was about "false imprisonment" for unpaid parking tickets or oppressive loitering laws, her letters to the editor exposed them as part of a larger plot to enslave the masses. Once, when she was about thirty, she paraded up and down the main street of her small, conservative hometown wearing a sandwich-board scrawled with clever anti-draft epithets. All I could think was how her mother must have felt! But Joan's mother was a very tolerant woman.

Her whole family seemed so broadminded compared to mine. She even had a brother who'd been a beatnik (something both Joan and I had dreamed we'd grow up to be). She not only had the siblings I'd longed for—she had the gall to have siblings who liked each other! When I admitted I was envious of her childhood in that free-thinking brainy household, she told me about the darker side.

"Every night there was a World War III argument over Kant or Hegel. My father would launch into a diatribe. The big boys would be shouting, the big girls crying, and my little brother and I would hide under the table.

"And the fist fights! God, they frightened me. My older brothers would roll across the floor, punching and pounding. When they were younger, they played cowboys and Indians, blasting each other with six-shooters. But, you know, they all grew up to be pacifists. And the kindest, smartest men I know! I guess you just can't tell what's going to shape us into what we become."

Well, from what I had seen of the world, Joan's family seemed the exception and not the rule. When I became the mother of a son, I had no experience with brothers to draw upon. But I soon began hearing about the proper New Age way to raise boys.

According to some people in my local community of liberal, middle-class, well-educated parents, there apparently existed a definite—if still unproven—correlation between violent play as a child and violence in adulthood.

Guns kill. Destruction is bad. Boys have to learn how to cooperate. Boys need to learn that violence is wrong. These were the New Age Commandments.

So who was I to disagree? I've always believed in peaceful negotiation—whether it's international or interpersonal. I'm even okay with being labeled a "Dove" in most situations.

But one day when Jack was almost three, something happened. We were walking through the park to his pre-school when he stopped to pick up a pretty pinecone. Sometimes he liked to have me bring them home for him to keep.

He scrutinized its detailed designs—and then we walked some more, until he stopped again to pick up a rock that interested him. And then, with his pinecone in one hand and his rock in the other, he began violently smashing them against each other over and over. He added the "Boom! Pow!" howls of destruction, along with a great big smile, and I knew we were on our way into a whole new territory.

I quickly formed the opinion that even if I still thought I could strongly influence Jack by what I nurtured in him, I'd be in gross denial if I made light of this new side of his nature.

Jack had never been very wild or boisterous, and he became obsessed with destruction games around the same time that he feared going on merry-go-rounds and kiddie trains.

The games he enjoyed most had to do with taking two of his toys—whatever they were—and pretending to smash, crash, explode and destroy them. Give him two toy cars and he would make sure they got in some kind of horrible, fiery accident. But that's where I came in.

I just had to intervene sometimes and explain to him that

the passengers inside the cars needed to be taken to the hospital as quickly as possible. Together he and I would make sure they got to our makeshift emergency room so we could bandage up the ones who'd lived through the trauma.

I thought it was good, and still do, to show him the other side—destruction does have its consequences. But then I'd leave his room, and the crashing, burning and fatal accidents would start all over again.

It's not as if Brian and I sat Jack in front of the TV all day and made him watch hours of violent TV shows. His enjoyment of destruction came to him as naturally as breathing, either from his genetic predisposition or from his being influenced by the kids he hung around with at school. Although, at his non-sexist, multi-ethnic, progressive pre-school, the small amount of aggressive play permitted was probably initiated by Jack as often as by his "violent" buddies.

Is destruction wrong only because it's man-made, and—I would have to add—boy-made? If so, were boys like my son barbarous, and did their inner natures have to be squelched? Is destruction really always bad?

I found it interesting to mull that one over. Vegetation is sometimes destroyed so sunshine can come in and allow other plants to grow. Fires can actually help a forest to flourish. Throughout history people have been hunting animals, chopping down trees, and damming rivers for good reason—to survive.

And what about *Mother* Nature with her volcanoes, avalanches, monsoons and earthquakes? It's true that people we love die. Even when strangers die, we usually feel terrible, and it's good that we care. But Mother Nature has to know what she's doing. Doesn't she?

Wars kill innocent people and cause great pain, but they've sometimes been a necessary last recourse for defending the weak and oppressed.

I told Jack that sometimes destruction and death were the way of things, but in many, many cases—not so good. I tried to advise him: You can smash up those empty soda cans, but do not destroy my computer. You can beat your rabbit puppet on the head with a bat all day if you want to. Do not hurt real live bunny rabbits. And so on.

Then his birthday came and all he wanted for presents were action hero figures. I knew mothers who wouldn't let their children have them. Action heroes condoned violence as a way of resolving conflicts, while we were trying hard to teach our kids to use their words instead of smacking each other. Jack's pre-school not only banned toy guns from the premises—but also action heroes—so the children would feel safe at school and not threatened or provoked by toys that represented violence.

This made some logical sense to me, though I didn't have strong feelings for or against. I just followed the rules. And then the day came when the teachers put their collective foot down. Action heroes' pictures were banned from lunchboxes.

As I stood at the kitchen counter peeling Batman's picture off Jack's new blue plastic lunchbox, I had to wonder if Batman was really all that bad. Identifying with him made Jack feel powerful and gave him a lot of pleasure.

Wouldn't anyone want to feel powerful if they were three or four and so small, having little control over such a huge world? But then I recognized my own attraction to Batman, and I had to look at that.

He was just my type—intelligent, kinda cute, involved with doing good, and evolved enough to use his God-given gifts to help people in need, rather than flaunting them for his own selfish ends.

Sure he punched people out, but I guess I could understand why he had to. People are so immoral! I could appreciate a guy like him doing good in a society where we're too often encouraged to be self-absorbed, and to dwell on how we look and whom we can impress by buying this or that and the hell with everybody else.

So at least Batman had a strong social conscience, which I believed to be his subliminal message. Yet he was still a "man's man," which I guess all those little boys could appreciate.

But even though I accepted Batman's violent tendencies, it wasn't without trepidation; and I just didn't have enough passion for his cause to protest his exile from school. So I pulled Batman's picture off of Jack's lunchbox, and that was that.

A few months later, at a birthday party for kids in Jack's class, the birthday boy's mom passed out "gender-specific" party favors at the end.

I only use those words because one of the dads used them. "My daughter didn't go for that gender-specific stuff—she put back the nail polish, and asked for the motorcycle!" Then he gave a big thumbs up.

I liked this man and appreciated his sincerity—his daughter at least thought for herself and knew how to go for what she wanted. But I couldn't help wondering—what if the roles had been reversed?

What if this man had a son who put back the mini motorcycle and went for the red nail polish? Would he say, "My son doesn't go for that gender-specific stuff!" and give a big thumbs up? Would any father in the world? Would I?

As a mother, I know if Jack were attracted to the nail polish, I would fear his life might immediately turn more difficult and painful. At the same time, many of us women have not been comfortable with the more typically "feminine" side of humanity being so undervalued. And to stay consistent, that even includes nail polish.

Nail polish is *not* silly. If it is, then a toy motorcycle is, too. So there!

There is absolutely nothing wrong with wanting to feel beautiful and desirable. The problem comes for me when looking beautiful becomes the top priority in life, when character is made light of and looks alone are used to impress people or make them feel lesser than.

So one day I got myself all worked up. What about Barbie? Why hadn't anyone ever suggested banning her from school and not allowing her picture on lunchboxes?

Barbies were strewn around Jack's pre-school all over the place. As if Barbie doesn't hurt people! Batman is at least trying to do the right thing, but what is Barbie trying to do?

I know there are Barbie doctors now, Barbie veterinarians or whatever, since we women have become so "liberated." But isn't the most important thing about her still *that body?* The fact she has great boobs and looks terrific while she's transplanting that pancreas!

As a girl I had insisted my mom buy me one for my birthday. But before Barbie and I were through, that doll had done her damage. Would I ever be able to look like her? How could I grow up to be *that* perfect? And that's what she made me want. Now I can't help but see her as being as violent as Batman in her own way.

Barbie just may have a subtle plan to kill our souls, or at the very least to belittle what is important about each of us. I'm also aware that I have an especially negative reaction to her. Jack just thinks she's goofy, but then—he's a boy.

Would I ever protest Barbies being brought to school? Never. I imagine that for a lot of girls, playing with Barbie serves a good purpose, even if it's personally hard for me to relate to it. And to ban anything anywhere that isn't physically dangerous has always made me nervous. No matter how small the situation, it still reminds me too much of the Nazi S.S. burning books.

But who's to say such a drastic action as prohibiting Barbies would even do any good? A national survey I read in *Time Magazine* showed that seventy-five percent of girls aged twelve to seventeen, whose baby boomer '60's and '70's parents had tried hard to instill in them anti-materialistic, humanitarian values, listed "supermodel" as the job they would most like to have when they grew up. There's nothing wrong with being a model, but aren't we also going to need some medical researchers or city planners?

Is our culture solely responsible for this? Or is it in a girl's nature—this longing to be beautiful and admired? I may be criticized for even suggesting that last question, but really, does anybody know?

Around the time I had to peel Batman off Jack's lunchbox, my cousin Beverly happened to buy him a large Star Wars' figure that came with a life-sized red toy gun. Even mothers I knew who let their children have action heroes stopped at toy guns. This was my first experience with one, and I have to say Jack seemed to get a lot out of pointing it at his toys, stuffed animals, action heroes and his mother, allowing him to feel moments of great power and a break from being told all day long what to do.

Yet I can't say I always felt completely at ease seeing him running around the house with a gun, so I told him that guns kill people, and that his gun was only okay because it wasn't real. That seemed all that was necessary.

What made me even more certain was a visit I had up in the Bay Area with Joan and Graham at her mother's house. Graham and Jack had been loudly playing in the next room, when Graham suddenly came darting past us with a three-foot long plastic shotgun.

"So, Joan, you let him play with guns?" I asked as he trailed away.

"He has so many of them at home. They just keep collecting. He gets tired of them," she laughed. "So he loves to play with the ones here." My shock settled into relief and I went back to munching my fudge brownie. Wasn't *that* interesting! Joan and I had found solid common ground in something I never would've predicted—our staunch indifference to boys and their guns!

One day Jack had a friend over, a boy with the strongest anti-toy gun, anti-action hero, anti-violence mother I'd ever met—the type who would never in a million years allow her son to own a *picture* of a toy gun. Just as she was leaving, the kids disappeared into Jack's bedroom, and in less than twenty seconds her son came tearing out the back, waving Jack's gun. Then he pointed it directly at his mom's face. I wanted to disappear.

How had he found it that fast among all Jack's stuff? I imagined from the shocked expression underneath his mother's uncomfortably polite smile that she thought Jack had a thousand guns and was a violent maniac.

Mostly I believed she thought I was a degenerate mother for not taking a strong stand on the matter. It was true. I wasn't even ambivalent. More bland. Not troubled. Confused is too big a word. Toy guns just didn't seem very harmful to me. Yet I thought something might be wrong with my nonchalant attitude.

Now some time has passed, and I see how Jack's existence has naturally encouraged me to explore issues from all sides, and that many of them seem far too complex to justify radical decisions or declarations. Others just don't seem that important.

In the modern, middle class world of raising children, parents expound many righteous beliefs. Sometimes I have them myself, but more often I don't.

I'm trying to accept that I may come off as wishy-washy, or not involved enough with Jack's welfare. But maybe it's all right for me not to take a stand on every single issue. Better instead to work at becoming more comfortable with admitting my indifference, like the fact that I've never come up with a sufficient reason—or cared about it enough—to take Jack's gun away.

IS IT FOR HIM
OR IS IT FOR YOU?

(or The World According to Guilt)

in which Joan earns a black and white belt in masochism...

At one and a half, Graham barely spoke five words, but he could imitate perfectly the sounds of every passing truck. I figured it must be some kind of ancient genetic programming to learn the cries of the mastodons and bison he would be hunting someday. So when his interest in guns took off at age seven, my resistance gave way. After all, in spite of my attempts to keep the daycare free of violence and sexism, Graham had already been exposed to gobs of behaviors I could not explain by way of developmental stages or ancestral memory.

"The word *hug* is so much prettier, Taylor. Let's sing it together—*I wanna hug you, baby...*"

"No! Das nodda way! *Wanna fuck you babeeeeee! Fuck you baybeeeeee!*"

As enlightened and experienced as I pretended to be, I found I was no match for the pure zen of the preschool mind. What was the appropriate response to: "C'mon, Amber! Let's stab ourselves in the heart so we can go to heaven right away!"

Pedagogical theory is so much easier than practice.

I envied Linda's ability to take human behavior in stride. At least most of the time she granted humankind the right to its own foibles. She had that wonderfully broad Aquarian overview of it all. I was the quintessential Pisces always getting in too deep. Maybe I took everything too seriously when it came to kids. That's why it had taken me forever to finally truly close the doors to my charity daycare. I think my new resistance to saying the word "Yes," surprised Linda when she called to ask if I'd go on a blind date with some friend of a friend of hers.

"He has kids!" she bubbled as if that gave him points.

"He has kids? I hate kids. Well, maybe that's too strong. I don't hate them. I still really think they're neat. In the abstract. I just don't want to be around them. Okay—not Graham. Not Jack. But the rest of them. I'm done. Right now I am so very done. It's dangerous to bring a kid near me. It is. I scare myself."

"Yeah, it's all quiet on your end—except for the birds. So you're not babysitting anymore?"

"Well, not now, anyway. I just don't know how much longer I can stretch my recovering-from-surgery excuse."

"You told them you had an operation?"

"Yeah. A hysterectomy."

"Wow, that's kind of a whopper. Why didn't you just tell them you couldn't afford to do it anymore or something?"

"Because I had a hysterectomy. So I thought—"

"You had a HYSTERECTOMY? When did you have a hysterectomy?

"In uh March."

"Oh."

Uh-oh. Linda's hurt. "What could you have done anyway? You're five hundred miles away."

"I would have made a trip up! You should tell me things like that."

"I'm telling you now! But Linda it was no big deal. I'm fine."

"Okay, I'm sending you some more steaks in the mail. For iron."

"I don't need iron now."

"Well, it's your fault. Now I have to send a retroactive care package."

"No. Don't," I insisted.

"Wow! Did you hear that?"

"What?"

"It was so easy for you to say no."

"Yeah, I said no. I don't want you to spend all that money on steaks. I'm not anemic anymore!"

"You're not mad at me, are you?"

Oh. God here we go. "No, I'm just. I guess I'm angry at myself. I always felt so sorry for all those moms who never got a break, just racing from work to pick up their kids and then racing home to report in for domestic duty. I felt so privileged to be able to be home. And I did want to help. For the parents, just giving them a little breathing room. For the kids, well, I hate to see them locked up all day in the local internment camp they call daycare up here. I felt like I was providing asylum, you know."

"But you deserve asylum, too."

"Yeah, I actually need to be in an asylum. Eventually you run out of steam being the mom with all the free time and no car to drive off and be unavailable in.

"Yeah, sounds like you don't really hate kids, you're just tired of being helpful, being the Village—"

"Idiot. Yeah."

"What happened?"

"I don't know. I think it was that thing you said about Thom winning the Monopoly game. I think it just gradually worked its way up to the surface."

"Wow! Sounds like worms when it rains or something."

I laughed. Hard. It was tough to stop.

Finally Linda spoke. "I haven't heard you laugh. I mean *laugh* that laugh, *your* laugh. Not since—well, since Graham.

I love it!"

I basked in Linda's approval. I was so high on it I said yes to the blind date. I wanted to live up to her faith in my ability to be more like her. I figured she still thought I was a doormat when it came to parenting, though. We were so different. She mothered like a butterfly, I like a hawk. We were different when it came to guilt, too. She swatted it whenever it came buzzing around. I usually curled up in its nest and hatched the offspring.

But when it came to questioning our credibility as mothers, we were in the same boat. We had enough surplus self-doubt to start a mail-order business. Motherhood seemed like a perpetual taboo factory. When last year's prohibition becomes obsolete, there's a new improved model to replace it. One thing we never had doubts about, though, was our devotion to our kids.

Well, what parent doesn't feel devoted to her child? In all the Bedlam of emotions and conflicting needs that come with parenting, devotion seems to hover above the tumult like an angel of instinct—part reason, part urge—with lofty wings and bloody teeth, so primal and pervasive parents take it for granted. Until someone questions it.

"Do you really think working every weekend is good for him?" or "Are you sure you should have custody, when your ex could give her a room of her own and a puppy?"

Sometimes we can just duck these accusations of selfishness. But if we're already feeling uncertain about our choices, such well-meaning advice can throw us onto a mobius strip of toxic reflection.

There are drawbacks to being a teenage unwed mother, but self-doubt is not one of them. At sixteen, I knew exactly what it took to be a good mother: breast-feeding, Parent Effectiveness Training and a well-worn copy of *Summerhill*. I couldn't always live up to my own lofty principles, but they stood firm along the rocky reefs of parenthood, towering like Easter Island statues of Abraham Maslow, A.S. Neill and Carl Rogers.

But years later when Graham was born, I was no longer young and over-confidant. My comfortable certitude crumbled, like any monolith to an ancient deity. I suddenly felt I didn't really *get* child-rearing.

Although the science of human development continued to sprout certified experts like weeds, I was still stumped. Experts speak in terms of *a* plus *b* equals *c*. What if you're dealing with f, q, n, and x—maybe the whole Greek alphabet as well?

Like most mothers, I took for granted the mass of inter-personal variables, complex psycho-dynamics, and Myers Briggs minutia my brain constantly recorded, processed and cataloged about my son's development. And like most mothers, I discounted this too subjective storehouse of knowledge as insignificant next to the objective precision of Science and the durability of Tradition.

Without creed or confidence, I had no hard and fast rules anymore—which made me an easy mark for those who did.

One afternoon, I joined my new friend, Mindy to watch her daughter's baseball practice. "You've got to sign Graham up. You'll love it, and he would have such fun!" Mindy was a lawyer and could be very persuasive, but never pushy. I knew she just wanted the best for my pathetically sports-deprived eight-year-old.

"Well, I just don't think Graham's interested." I answered, as I watched him jump off a swing into the sand. "I ask him every year, and he doesn't seem to want to." Oops, my Fritz Perls was showing!

Maybe all that right brain touchy-feely stuff was a bunch of archaic hooey! In the Post-Aquarian Age I was probably supposed to *demand* that Graham claim his birthright as an American and play ball!

"Graham could have so many friends if he joined a team, and you can't be a buffer for him forever." Mindy waved to another mom as we lugged the heavy cooler to the bleachers.

"Yeah, I know that. Where's Sheila?" I smiled, trying to change the subject.

"You know, Joan," she sat down to face me as if I were a puppy who'd peed on her carpet. "You really have to ask yourself—are you keeping him out of sports for him—or for *you?*"

I deflected the subtle jibe with a nod of pensive consideration. But what a stupid question! Of course it was for him!

Trusting Graham's choices to play in his own un-organized, non-competitive way was one of the few aspects of mothering I felt confident about. I didn't want to push him to compete.

I certainly understood the competitive urge. But when it came to Little League—well, there was just something about Little League. Even Linda's and Jack's hearty enthusiasm for it had not entirely dispelled my suspicion that it was a secret grange hall brotherhood devoted to breeding rabid nationalists.

As a child I'd managed to enjoy a few years of competitive swimming, despite the constant teasing I got, which, contrary to Nietzsche's over-used epithet, had not made me stronger—only confused, disgusted and even more sensitive. My daughter had played soccer all through elementary school, enduring similar problems.

Oh my god! What a pile of obviously *personal* objections! Apparently I did have a stake in this! Maybe Mindy was right. Maybe I was supporting Graham's sports apathy—at least partly—*for me.*

Trying to avoid eye contact with Mindy, I stared across the field and caught sight of Sheila, sitting on a bench, her head in her hands. She seemed to be sobbing. "What's the matter with Sheila?" I asked.

"Oh, she does that," Mindy called over her shoulder as she

yanked six-packs out of the cooler. "The last two seasons she just sat on the bench and cried. But I know she'll play this year. They get used to it."

For a moment the second hand in my brain wouldn't move. I had only met Mindy a few weeks before, but I'd seen how protective she was of Sheila—no sugar, no Barbies, no PG movies. Yet somehow she interpreted her daughter's tearful resistance as a plea for another year of encouragement, while I saw it as a neon billboard to bail.

The question suddenly flashed into my mind: *Was baseball for Sheila or was baseball for Mindy?* Could Mindy be forcing her daughter to follow in her own highly competitive footsteps? Or did Mindy perhaps remember crying on the sidelines as a little girl, and her parents bolstering her self esteem by cheering her on? Maybe she was trying to recreate the support she'd received as a child, in which case, *she was doing it for Sheila.*

I let the baseball issue slip down into the quagmire of doubt I carried around like a pail of slop. But soon it began to fester. I'd always believed it was important to examine one's motivations. Maybe I hadn't looked deep enough. Linda and I had always felt that the deeper you went the closer you got. Perhaps it was time to hop into the psychic diving bell and try out this new detective tool on my hidden motives.

For him or for you? Well, as tools go, this one was a gem. Perhaps the first empirically objective standard for distinguishing between good mothering and bad! A perfect mantra for the guilt-ridden! Not messy and ambiguous like family therapy or esoteric and impractical like Rudolf Steiner's mysticism. As convenient as a Cosmo test, as versatile as duct tape—it seemed to possess the wisdom of Solomon. Was I doing what truly suited Graham's needs or was I just falling back on what the ever-present Voice of Shame told me was my slovenly selfishness?

Surely this mood ring for the conscience could eliminate all that waxy build-up of self doubt, giving me whiter whites and blacker blacks till I could see my old certainty shining back at me.

While these thoughts bobbed in the swill of my dissolving child-rearing philosophies, I stumbled onto another learning experience and realized that condemnation knocks twice.

It was the blind date Linda had set up for me. *The really neat guy with kids.*

Although I was shaking, and sweating like a fountain, I managed to give the hipster-architect potential suitor a goofy "written exam" to break the ice. Then, gripping our mugs of tea for dear life, we settled down to explore our commonalities.

Politics and social views clicked. So on we went, edging gingerly down that slippery slope of personal disclosure until we arrived at the more intimate subject of our children. I told him I'd been very nervous about homeschooling at first, but that now I was enjoying it.

"The question is," he pronounced looking very wise in his shiny goatee, "are you're doing it for him or for *you*?" Oh, the stench of déjà vu!

Like a pudgy cartoon bullet, the question spiraled toward me in slow motion. If only I could leap and roll out of its path, dodging the oncoming implication like Steven Segal in an exploding warehouse of moral dilemmas.

Finally, grasping at any polite straw of social convention, I mustered a giggle. "Oh yes, I ask myself that all the time." But I knew full well my confession about *"enjoying it"* had already done me in. I suppose if I'd said, *"I'm home-schooling my son and you can't imagine how much I despise every minute of it!"* well, then there'd be no doubt about my selfless motives.

But wedding bells were never meant to chime for that father of two girls in boarding school and this mother of an eight-year old boy hogtied in apron strings. Maybe Linda had just wanted to remind me there were other things in life besides child rearing. Yes, the blind date had brought all that back with crystal clarity, and I knew full well that after hollowing myself out to make a shell for my son to live in, I perhaps didn't bring a lot to the table of matrimonial conviviality.

I decided to turn my fear and confusion outward. I would call Linda, pour out all my distress and blame her for it.

"But Joan...post traumatic stress disorder? It happened five minutes ago." She hated feeling that she'd caused anyone pain. If I didn't immediately reassure her I was fine, the conversation would swiftly turn into a comfort session for Lindaand not me.

"Then I'm having present traumatic stress disorder. But it's nobody's fault. Except maybe his."

"Yeah, he probably felt threatened by you," she said.

"Threatened by me?"

"Yeah, that you don't do what he does, so it makes him think either you've gotta be wrong or he's gotta be wrong."

"That man does not ever think he's wrong!"

"I don't know, but let's face it, Joan, there's a big mistake about what you're doing."

"Mistake?"

"MystEEK."

"You said mistake."

"No, I said: mystEEK, as in feminine mystique."

"No, you said MISTAKE. You said, 'There's a big mistake about what I'm doing'."

"No, I didn't say that!" she blustered. "Why would I—? I said there's a big mystique about homeschooling. It's true. It's—well, it can seem very intimidating to other people."

"Intimidating?"

"Sure," her voice became a bit strident. "You stay home, you sacrifice—you don't do things you used to do. When you first told me, I didn't like it. It made me feel kinda irresponsible compared to you. Until you told me how you did it. That's what took away the mystique. I could see you weren't really that super devoted goddess. You were just..."

"—a mess."

"You're not a mess! It just seems like you're giving so much to Graham and there's nothing left over for you. I don't know."

"Oh." I heaved out one gigantic sob. "I don't know who I'm doing anything for anymore. God! What do you say when people ask you that, "Is it for him or for you?"

"Um... well, I don't think anyone's ever—" she tried to soften the absurdity, "ever really had to ask me that."

I hung up, wrung out. No. Linda's enemies, internal or external, would never attack her on that front. Why would anyone bother to accuse Linda of being selfish? She was! And proud of it, well most of the time. I was the perfect sucker for this Chinese finger puzzle of the mind. I knew I should relax, stop struggling against the internal accusation that only gripped me tighter as I tried to escape.

Maybe I should have let the architect—Heck—let everyone see my resentful side. *"I can't go anywhere without him. Not even outside to the front porch! Do you think I find that personally fulfilling?"* In fact maybe my resentment was the solution to the dilemma itself. Maybe it would be wise to qualify all my motherly obligations in this way, lest someone think I am hemming Graham's pants *for me!* Or frying up his twelfth egg burrito of the day *because it's such a gas.* Or searching through a box of ten thousand Lego pieces for the "yellow guy's arm" *to satisfy my lust for adventure.*

"Let there be no doubt," I could now shout to the world, "all those kids' places I take my son to—pizza parlors, public pools, Good Humor trucks, birthday parties—I hate them! Yes! I would spurn them all if it weren't for my son! So proudly I declare myself pure in my devotion and untainted by selfish interest! Yes, it's all for him and none for me!"

Wow, this simple shibboleth might mean the end to all my self-doubt as a mother. After all, it only had two categories. There was absolutely no anxiety-producing middle ground. Hey—maybe I could use this handy motivation-detector to quantify all my parenting. And I might score better now that I was a stay-at-home mother simply due to the extra twelve hours a day I had at my disposal to be selfless in!

I'd always wondered why so many working-outside-the-home parents seemed to think all we stay-at-home-parents did was give and nurture and sacrifice. Obviously a baseless prejudice.

Still, now I began to wonder if I'd been selling myself short. Maybe I was giving more than I thought I was. But let the *Martyr Meter* decide! God, my self-esteem might be through the roof by the end of the day!

6:00 AM Get up before Graham, make coffee, fill the four by six foot blackboard with my expressionist interpretation of man's evolution from hunter to farmer. *For him or for me?* Okay, so he hates history. But capturing an anthropological crescendo in pastels makes me happy and isn't a happy mother a—*never mind. Forfeit this round.*

7:00 Graham is up and working on his computer. Wants my help reading difficult words. *For him or for me? For him!* Absolutely! Well, except that I love helping him learn to read. *Okay, no gold stars yet.*

8:30 Yoga. More my thing than his. Puts me below zero, but I'll catch up.

9:00 Dungeons and Dragons. We both love it. So the *for me* cancels out the *for him.*

10:00 Science experiment—another net wash.

11:00 Tennis. This is going nowhere!

12:00 Make lunch. Finally! A good solid *Definitely His!* Although—gosh, if he starved, how would that make *me* feel?

No, I was just looking out for Number One again.

1:00 Graham invites a friend over. Okay, this should do it. Now, as much as I like Graham's friends, and children in general, I could never say that I invited his friends over to fulfill *my* needs! Oh, Heck, I forgot how intensely gratifying it is to see Graham happy. I give up. It really is all about me.

Wait! How about standing that ruler on its head. Surely I could score a few points for selflessness if I consider all the bad things I'm *not doing*. That's probably where I realy shine as a mother—being so over-protective and all!

Let's put a big blue ribbon around all those things I would never ever do, even if they might make my life a bit easier. Like apprenticing him to a wandering dung peddler. Or dragging him around with me on a Lost Weekend binge. Or turning him over to the California Youth Authority.

Ahh. Now that feels good! Real good! *But hold on! Don't crack open that champagne yet!* What about all those *nice* things I'm not doing for him, like camping out and going to amusement parks?

Although Graham shared my distaste for such self-abuse, I wondered if boyhood was really complete without vomiting upside down inside a loop-de-loop. And what about camping? The unswerving code of For Him or For Me might include what's *for his own good*. Now, up here in the woods, camping is only a little less patriotic than burning a pile of Hilary Clinton's books. So maybe that was one obligation I had to fulfill in order to prove my selfless devotion. But since Graham and I already lived with mountain lions, rattlesnakes, bears, leaks in the roof and neighbors who solved conflicts with chainsaws—weren't we really sort of full-time campers?

Some would say that didn't count. Apparently lying in a soggy tent, being eaten by mosquitoes and covered with ants was a necessary right of passage, the neglect of which placed me in the negative numbers on that devil's yardstick some-where between Andy Warhol and Katherine the Great.

Why was I such a failure at selflessness? Because I got too much vicarious gratification from my child's well-being, I suppose. But isn't that the key nature provides to help us through this difficult career?

The same empathy that makes the stomach cramp when our children cry also makes the heart soar when they laugh. Can we really even tell where the *for him* stops and the *for me* begins?

Maybe a robot could offer a pure *all-for-him* child rearing. A robot would be incapable of selfishness. A robot would also be incapable of self-doubt. But for human children, maybe it's not so bad—maybe it's even necessary—to be exposed to the self-doubt that makes us truly human.

Certainty can teach us how to how to march in place, but not how to move forward. I guess I prefer interpretive dance. Maybe that's the beauty of self-doubt.

WAXING NOSTALGIC
FOR MY HOME PLANET

(or Confessions of a Self-Indulgent Mother)

in which Linda manages to suffer over avoiding suffering...

Guilt and *motherhood* go together like *American* and *apple pie*, don't they? Well, they did for Joan. But I've never been able to get motivated by guilt the way some people can. There are times I've wished I could, just so I wouldn't feel like such an oddball.

Sometimes I feel like I don't belong on Earth. It has mainly to do with not fitting in, but it's also about *not always wanting* to fit in.

So many women I know dream of buying a house. But when Brian and I finally put a down payment on a two bedroom place, I found myself almost repelled. Everyone was exuberant with profuse congratulations. Everyone except Joan. Maybe she sensed my ambivalence.

"Buying a house can make you feel so imprisoned. It can really dominate your life, and kind of suck up your energy."

"Like a child?"

"Touché," she grumbled.

I didn't mean to make Joan feel guilty, but I'd certainly felt pushed out of her life after she had Graham. "It's not like I'm imprisoned—I don't think," I went on. "I just feel my mother."

"You feel like your mother?"

225

"No, I *feel my mother*—in buying the house."

"It's like your mother's—yeah—your *mother's* house!"

"No! I like the house. But maybe I'd rather not own it. It's buying the house—having it. I just feel my mother in all of that. That's what she wanted for me."

"Ohhhh."

"Yeah, my security mattered so much to her, in such an extreme way. And now I have it. But I don't feel like congratulating myself. Maybe my mom. But not me. I feel funny—it's like living inside the dream she had for my future."

"Right. Of course." She stammered with uncertainty. I could hear her trying too hard. It was arousing my feelings of being wrong. I finally made an excuse to hang up because I knew I couldn't explain it so Joan would really understand. And how could she? Coming from that damned supportive family of hers! And if Joan couldn't understand, nobody could. I was up to my neck in alienation.

As deeply as I loved my mother, I had sometimes wondered if I were adopted, as many children do. But after awhile the feeling of coming from a different family expanded till I was pretty sure I'd come from a different planet. I could have labeled myself a genetic mutant, but that would have cut off all hope. I wanted to believe that somewhere there were others like me.

Back when I'd first met Joan, that feeling was at an all-time high. I'd just quit my lucrative job as a rehabilitation counselor and become a waitress to devote more time to writing. But I never told my father about it. He died two years later, content in the knowledge that his daughter had put her silly creative urges behind her and was holding down an important job—a job that made her somebody he wanted to brag about. Maybe I was wrong to lie, but why shouldn't he die happy?

After waitressing for a year, I followed Joan's lead and

took up temping. Better money, less commitment. Pretty soon Joan and I were both working wearisome secretarial jobs in San Francisco's Financial District. At Happy Hour we'd get together to work on our screenplay, a project I was determined to shape into a commercial success.

Its personal significance as a story about a foreigner in a strange new world didn't hit me until the night we celebrated Joan's awards for her Esperanto art film about an alienated word-processor. Then it all made sense. Both films were about the same wretched angst!

I told Joan about this feeling of being from somewhere else. "I love that!" Joan gasped, pounding her fist on the little table, jostling the egg rolls. "It gives you permission to honor the way you are! Your customs, sort of. They're not crazy or wrong! They're just foreign to the world you've been transplanted to. Somewhere in some unknown world, who and how you are is completely normal."

"Yeah," I answered without enthusiasm. "Thanks, but I live here."

"Oh, that's right. You're exiled or expatriated or something."

"But that's too respectable. It feels more like I'm bad. I'll never belong."

"Yeah. Well, your nonindigenous! I wish we could get you back to your own planet. I'd go with you. Just think—we could be as frightened and mixed up as we wanted, and everyone would just smile and nod knowingly! Immigrants would take re-sensitivity training so they could fully benefit from their liberation from repression. We could call it LindaLand!"

"Or Joan'stown," I laughed.

No matter how thoroughly Joan honored my sense of alienation, it didn't make me feel any better. When I felt this way, Joan was just another Earthling—who happened to love me.

More than anything else I felt misunderstood. But it was

comforting to imagine that people back on my home planet completely understood me (unlike Earth people) so at least I had a support group—albeit in a galaxy far, far away.

Since I'd felt like an outsider since I was a child, I'd always hoped it would just disappear one day; that perhaps I'd grow out of it.

Back when I was single, I imagined starting a family would make me feel more a part of this society of Earthlings. As it turned out, I never felt more like I didn't belong here than when I became a mother. Not that I didn't want to share in this great new world of parenting. I wanted and needed to learn everything I could, but the answers I was getting never seemed to fit the questions I was asking.

When Jack was just a baby I read in a parenting advice book about how important it was to spend time with your child every day in order to bond, to make him feel safe, and to let him know you care.

At the time it seemed an almost too obvious bit of advice. But even now I still find myself asking, *HAVE YOU SPENT ENOUGH TIME WITH JACK TODAY?* The words glide by like the "HAPPY NEW YEAR!" readout at Times Square.

I glance back as they trail by, give them a quick nod, and think—well, I'm not positive I've really spent enough time with Jack, but I probably have—and then I keep on going.

Actually, I never spend enough time with anybody. At least not the kind of time I'd like. There's always so much to do.

Whenever I finally do get around to calling Joan or any of my other friends—none of whom I ever spend enough time with—up flies the banner streaming across my mind again, reminding me of my maternal obligations.

I see it when I want to be alone with Brian for a while, or alone with myself to write, or to simply lie down and read a magazine. *HAVE YOU SPENT ENOUGH TIME WITH JACK TODAY?* I half expect a follow-up to this unrelenting yellow alert. *"STAY TUNED FOR ALARMIST ADVISORIES ON CONSEQUENCES OF GO-FISH DEPRIVATION."*

I brush it away like a mosquito. Maybe that's it! My insufficient maternal guilt is just more evidence that something *is* wrong with me. It's so easy for me to take care of my own needs without fretting that I'm neglecting Jack's. Could I be outside the normal human range of selfishness?

But those selfish needs are what keep me within the normal human range of sanity. For me, the fear of losing myself overshadows everything else.

Next to the obligations of motherhood, the need for self-expression may seem superfluous. But mine is more like a survival instinct. It's as intense as physical pain. I have to respond to it—or die. So giving myself time to focus on creative endeavors hasn't been very hard for me compared to many mothers I know. This lack of conflict over attending to my needs has made me feel apart from my own kind. Strange. And wrong.

Many women seem able to express their creativity through raising children. Parenting *is* their artform. They shouldn't be forced to take a drawing class or audition for a community theatre role.

But my vehicle is writing. If I spend too much time away from it, I do feel wanting. I do suffer. And, unlike the traditional motherhood model, I'm a lousy sufferer.

I've read articles in parenting magazines reminding us moms to take time for ourselves, and that's when I've really felt different. I have to wonder—just who are they talking to? Obviously, not the *Happy Hedonist*.

If only I *were* one of those extremely devoted mothers who had to be reminded! Those selfless and devoted women, so wrapped up in their kids they don't notice they haven't eaten for two days. I'm more like the wire monkey in those maternal deprivation experiments.

Actually, most mothers I know complain about never having enough time for themselves or their husbands or their friends—it seems to be a universal problem for mothers of young children. And then there's me—completely taking advantage of Jack for being an easy kid, and my only one.

Apparently, I have the world's lowest threshold for suffering. Self-expression seems to be my master gauge, regulating all other physical, mental and emotional systems. When that dial's on empty, nothing else goes. I know self-sacrifice is noble and worthwhile, but for me, even a little too much of it is like sugar to a diabetic.

There seems to be a single rhythm that beats at the heart of every parenting book or article, a rhythm I cannot master— and that's, of course, that your child *always comes first*. And only if he or she is perfectly comfortable and content, should you slip away—even into the next room to take a bubble bath. But what mother alive could ever arrange her life so perfectly?

And are we supposed to try? My new house felt like it was trying. Trying to be perfect. Just the way it was all supposed to be—in my mother's dream for my life. I felt as if I were a doll in her dollhouse. Owning a house meant I was living at the end of her rainbow. Maybe that's why she couldn't tolerate my own dreams. They threatened to derail me from the one true path to happiness. A safe, secure and affluent home.

I realized soon enough that my house required some serious breaking in. I would never feel I belonged here if I let my mother's old dreams take hold of the place.

I decided I would have to liberate it: turn it into my cultural center, my consulate of diplomatic immunity from the rules of an alien world, a place where the Old Planet Ways of Tolerance and Self-expression ruled. And that probably meant ritually breaking some of those quaint earthling customs right away— especially the ones about repressing your own needs till the "right time."

So I decided to start small and work my way out. I would

begin at the eye of the storm. My computer. I would claim this territory in the name of militant self-indulgence. Not that I was about to set the Hollywood Hills ablaze with flaming letters: "MY CHILD COMES SECOND!" Nor would I need to embroider a pillow to silently nag, "Have you spent any time with yourself today?" No. All I really needed was a homely wooden plaque inscribed with the bureaucratic prerogative: *All Needs Will Be Considered in the Order in which They Were Received.*

Oh, no, here he comes. The door swings wide and the hall light spills in. His tiny body, silhouetted like a lone gunfighter, fills the doorway, casting its towering shadow of needs across the floor. I'm already ankle deep.

No play dates are set up for Jack and he's bored. He doesn't usually use the word "bored" around me because he knows I consider it a profanity. I've told him he has too many toys, too much imagination, and it's too big a world for him to ever be bored.

"I can't find anything to do." The demand behind the innocent words hits me like a poisoned arrow, *You're his Mom! Get up and do something about it! You can't be too busy for your son!*

I rise from my chair, but the call of my ancestors pulls me back. *Now hold on! Let's not be hasty!* cries the Greek Chorus from the Old Planet. *You ARE too busy! Defend the hill!*

So without lifting my head from the computer screen, I grit my teeth, rasping out a "Jack, look harder," as I continue struggling with the phrase I need to type. *Her voice was— what? —frenzied? —frantic? —frenetic?*

For a while I have to put up with Jack's restlessness, and with blaming myself for not taking him to the park or an enriching children's museum on a beautiful warm Saturday afternoon—which I might want to do if I weren't writing. Then suddenly I hear him yelling and laughing, completely involved with the imaginary people he's found in his room. And all is well, at least for the time being.

Parenting isn't the only obstacle. I've found I'm only able to write for long periods if I'm really lost in what I'm doing. Even so, I'm hounded by self-doubt, and tempted by the escapist urge to get up and find something to scrub. Mostly I write between short therapeutic catnaps, like a boxer between rounds.

And then there's Brian to consider. Has he had to watch Jack more than me this week? Is it fair that he watches Jack again this evening? If I could write when Jack and Brian were in bed, it would be great. But then I'm too exhausted myself.

The best time is morning, but then I'm at work. So I write afternoons and weekends when Jack is playing like a wild man around the house, adding outer distractions to my inner demons.

The demand for meals and snacks is the usual interruption. But you have to feed your kid, don't you?

So there I am at the computer in the middle of a thought, and I hear him call out, "Mom! I'm hungry!"

Okay. I can handle this. Just because I'm finally living in the home my mother always dreamed I'd have does not mean I've moved into Harper Valley. "In a minute, Sweetie!" I put him off. I can feel the ancestors patting me on the back, "Attagirl!"

But my fingers hover as I am pulled by a morbid vision of my mother as a Jewish Betty Crocker in a steaming kitchen, baking and baking and baking to cover the stench of a hubby's disgrace. She wipes her bloody stumps across a cheery yellow apron and beckons me to hurry into my dream kitchen to make a dream sandwich and wax the dream floor. *No. Don't go into the light.* I force my recoiled fingers back to the keyboard. *Now, where was I? Oh, yes. But I can't use "ubiquitous" again so soon. Urgggh. Hmmm.*

"Mommy, I'm hungry!" I hear again. *Eek.* It's time for his

lunch. I realize it's been ten minutes since the last time he called me. Okay, I'm coming—but to my own real and imperfect kitchen, thank you. Just let me finish this paragraph—otherwise I'm going to forget. And of course, the time goes by.

"Mommy!" He pushes my door open, comes into the room, and sidles up to the computer with a frustrated look. "I need something to eat."

"Oh, God, I'm sorry, Jack. You've already asked three times. Let's go find something!"

Off we go to the kitchen, and do I go for the nutritious meal? No. I think, what is the fastest possible thing I can hand off to him so I can get right back to writing or else I'll never be able to figure out what it was I was trying to say.

Let's see. "There's some potato chips on the table, Sweetie, and I'll get some juice. And have a piece of this nice roll from last night! I'll get you something better pretty soon. I promise!" For a split second I think, boy, what a lousy mom, and then I rush back to the computer to get out the rest of the paragraph.

No, I haven't been so neglectful all the time. Just when I've needed to finish a thought. Shouldn't every mother be given that much slack? I decided then and there that the decorating motif for this house of mine should be *slack!* Perhaps I was carrying on the ancient traditions of my true foremothers. I longed to be back on my home planet, where people take quite seriously their need to express themselves, and everybody feels just fine about it. But for now I had planted my Freak Flag here—on this sometimes inhospitable planet.

I'm sure all of us feel weird and different sometimes. If I hadn't known Joan, I might never have believed another soul could understand how strange I felt. I thought she was humoring me, though, when she said she *learned* from my prodigious variety of emotional needs. "Linda, you're a transparent test tube of psycho-drama. After listening to you, I finally *get* things I never *got* before."

Hmmm. My incompetence at repression was becoming more of an asset, it seemed. Especially if Joan thought it truly was. Would that "learning" from me pay off and give Joan and itch she couldn't put off scratching? This inability to "squelch myself" has often seemed obnoxious to me, and probably to others, too. But not when I imagine the people on my home planet doggedly cheering me on.

I want to believe it's all right to tend to my own needs even if others piously forgo theirs. I want to believe it's my own business who comes first and when. And I'll be damned if I'm going to feel guilty!

From what I can tell, my short periods of temporary neglect haven't done Jack much harm. I don't think he's ever noticed he doesn't always come first. As unnaturally high as I often place my own needs, maybe second place really isn't all that shabby.

Jack's a basically happy, likeable kid who enjoys life and has great friends. Teachers and other parents say nice things to me about him. I like him too.

Sure, I probably should be taking him to more extracurricular classes and weekend afternoon events, but I've needed the time to write. Still, everything actually seems to be working out well—not in spite of my need to create—but maybe, actually, because of it!

Now I hear something. It's Jack. Madly rearranging his bedroom, turning it into a coliseum battle between the forces of good and evil. I hear his cries of *Fire* and *Go men!* and the mighty *thwap* of cardboard sword against wooden block monsters. The mayhem is music to my ears. Maybe he's doing just fine with my low key mothering. My need for "personal-expression time" may have rubbed off on him, or at least given him the time alone to let his own creativity run wild. Rationalization or not, I like it. Could this self-indulgence of mine actually be my legacy to him?

MISSING PERSON

(or The Nine Year Itch)

*in which Joan leaves her self on top of the car
and drives off...*

Mother's Day is traditionally the day I want to ask somebody
to lock me in a room and not let me out no matter how much
I howl. Linda had listened to me rag on it over the years. But
she would never feel it stab her in the back the way it did me.
Linda seemed to have an immunity to resentment. Deep down
I knew why. If you keep doing what you love, there's no room
for resentment. But I was not Linda. I was digging a cellar and
putting in a pool table to make resentment more comfortable.

It was my first Mother's day as a single mother again (the
annual Pon Farr boiling in my veins) when the guinea pig died.
The funeral arrangements kept me focused on grief and away
from self-pity.

Graham and I buried Torgo in the garden. We tossed flowers and recited a poem over the little grave. That's when
Graham started shrieking.

"He can't bweeve! He has to bweeve! Let him out!"

I quickly exhumed the body, and pretending to blow into
the sealed jaws, tried to convince him that Torgo didn't need
air anymore. But as I wrenched the clinging dirt clods from
its fur, I saw in that flattened, matted pelt something horrify-
ing. Something pathetic. My *self.* That wild, instinctual self

I'd buried so far down it couldn't bweeve! Flinging it into the iris, I grabbed my son and rocked him. But I could feel the hot breath of stale grief on my neck.

My unfinished mourning was always looking for a way in, and Torgo had ripped grief a new portal. As Cerberus, Lord of The Dance, he now led a jostling, weaving conga line of my recently departed. Through the rift they writhed, sounding off like dark Musketeers, "I'm Johnny! And I'm still waiting for you to let go!"

But the *baba-looing* ghost chain is just a warm-up act for the solo headliner. Now Torgo struts into the limelight and belts out a torch song. And I feel the dread. Full strength for the first time. The fear that I will never get back on that old home-made Loco Motive of my pre-birth dream. That I will never write another pretentious word. That I will never *bweeve* again.

If I never resuscitated that stifled passion, I knew it wouldn't be due to something as simple as writer's block. I only wished some kind soul had blown out my fifth chakra with a tranquilizer gun. No, my creative expression-compulsion remained. Dammed up by fears of my own dark side, it had amassed enough force to power an inner hydroelectric plant of displacement. Sublimated energy fueled round-the-clock puppet theatre, a felt toy cottage industry, and hydraulic excavation projects that would put the Army Corps of Engineers to shame.

I never had regrets about how I was raising Graham. He needed the fairytale world martyrdom had wrought. But as the years plodded on, as I got older and older, I wondered how long I could ignore that wax figure in the basement, frozen in time as if awaiting a future technology that could bring it back to life.

Well, evidently, I could wait a long time. Eventually there was no more conflict between creative drive and maternal duty. I no longer had to worry that history could repeat itself, that

I might neglect Graham the way I felt I had my first two children. Graham's neediness would continue to protect me from that. I'd found at least a superficial peace in channeling all my creative energy into motherhood, and I was coming to believe: I parent, therefore I am. Thus rang out the final death knell for my individuality.

Or did it? The psyche does not give up easily. Soon I had the first in a series of recurring dreams that visited me every night for the next three years.

It was about a man. A sort of nebulous, unfinished man. Radiant with soft energy. Perhaps he was not fully incarnated. Or was he made of wax? I wondered if he needed me to breathe life into him.

At the beginning of the dream I never seemed to know him. But he always recognized me, beckoning with a gentle, innocent smile. When I saw his eyes warm with deep unconditional love, I realized I had always known him. A saturating flood of joy let me know I would marry him.

I imagined this unfinished man must be the creative part of me, waiting for the time when I would invite him back into my life—the time we could complete each other. I woke in a cloud of euphoria that broke into a downpour. It was too soon. Graham needed me. But every night Unfinished Dream Man beckoned.

As the years went by, I began to wonder if I should stop pining away for him. I'd already enjoyed more opportunities for self-realization than most people would get in a lifetime. Why couldn't I be satisfied with that?

When Linda called and said she wanted to stay at my house in Dutch Flat this July on her annual visit to the Bay Area, my insides began to stir with fluttery anticipation—and with something else—something heavy and murky, like an undead passion rising from the grave.

I was thrilled when she arrived, and showed her around

the fantasy funhouse that was my Alpha and Omega. But Linda didn't *ooh* or *ah*. In fact, she looked disturbed. After I took her upstairs, I knew why.

It was suddenly so obvious to me that the only grown-up furniture in the place amounted to two dining room chairs. All five rooms were packed with children's playthings. There was not even one small corner of private adult space. I was seeing my quaint Gold Rush cottage through her eyes now— a nearly foundationless megalith of martyrdom, sagging under the weight of its burden, as ready to cave in as I was.

Linda set down her things and hugged me. It was a long embrace with extra sympathy/hold the judgment—the way I liked it. I felt embarrassed about my showcase of self-denial, and quickly asked her about Brian and Jack. Then she asked how I'd been. To anyone else I could have easily and convincingly answered, "Just fine!" But not to Linda. Not now. I choked up and finally stuttered, "I think I should be writing." Linda hugged me, then clapped her hands and jumped up and down like a toy monkey.

I stared at her in wretched ambivalence. I knew what really sickened me was the growing fear that time was passing— almost a decade had flown by. What if I never got to work on a project with Linda again? There had always been a special creative synergy between us. I missed being half of that dynamic duo.

The years never seemed to change Linda. She was just as funny, charming and well-informed as ever. Head still a little too big for that waif-like body. A life-size Cupie doll.

But I must have seemed very different to her—my gray earth-mother hair hanging down to what used to be a waist. I felt as tired as I looked. A poster child for entropy.

My cultural life took place inside the Bookmobile, and the only current event I was on top of was Cupcake's latest litter. I knew that I'd been stopping up my life flow. And I knew what I had to do to get its started again. But I couldn't let myself start something I might be unable to stop. When Linda left the next day, it seemed so final. I hoped I could cram all the feelings she'd aroused back into that little box marked DO NOT OPEN TILL GRAHAM'S THIRTIETH BIRTHDAY. But Unfinished Dream Man would not give up his wooing.

That winter, practicality reared her ugly head. Since I had closed the daycare, money was becoming a bigger and bigger problem. I began selling my child-sized furniture piece by piece. But how long could that go on? I knew anyone else peeking into my life would scoff at my dilemma. "You idiot! Get a job. Put the kid in school! He'll survive." Logical, responsible, pragmatic. But that didn't make it right.

After a nine-year run of Sublimation Theatre, I was at rock bottom, financially and emotionally. Then, only a few weeks after her visit, Linda called with her Big Idea. She got right to the point. Like a repression-smiting angel she delivered me from the temptation of common sense. We were going to "write a book together. It'll be fun!"

I nodded my encouraging uh-huhs into the phone as she went fervently on about "feelings women have," "mothers trying too hard," and "if nothing else, we'll feel better."

"Sure. It sounds great!" I had to force it out. The idea sounded bland and vague and utterly unmarketable. I didn't get it, but I didn't have to. I trusted Linda. She had a keen sense for how the seemingly inconsequential impacted the big picture of the human predicament. Linda could see beyond—or maybe even through—the world I saw.

I hung up—as thrilled, confused and guilty as if she'd asked me to rob a Catholic novelty store. This was the excuse I'd been waiting for! It was just the thirty-ton shove I needed. Ten years after my nervous breakdown, I was finally witnessing a jail break in my brain. As if that Bastille of threat perception had been stormed and rivers of prisoners were flooding out, lighting up both sides of my brain like a Christmas tree. I knew Graham would lose a little of my 24/7 attention, but I only had to convince myself he could benefit financially. Some day. A delusion, but a useful one. It was an excuse that had seen me through a couple decades, but did I really buy it anymore? Wasn't it too obviously just a cover for doing what I wanted? The case of Desire versus Denial would have to be brought before my Inner House of Commons.

"The Linda argument tires me. Ms. Cohen squanders time stolen from motherly duties to scribble out her pathetic manifesto," an old shrew droned at the podium. "Is this worthy of imitation?" When she whacked a ruler across the back of my head, I recognized my eighth grade teacher, Miss Harris. "If Linda threw her son off the Empire State Building, would that necessitate an immediate copy-cat response from Joan?"

"Honorable colleagues, we're comparing apples and oranges here." Oh, dear god, it's the Anal Master of Uniformity, my second husband! Fanning his sweaty face with a Bible, he circumambulates the massive statue of the Übermütter. "Jack and Graham are practically different species. Therefore, a dilettante mother of the first party might incur far less grievous consequences than a dilettante mother of the second party. And besides," he pointed at me now, "that bitch was always trying to poison me!"

From the back of the dark-paneled room came a quavering voice, "But what about her need for self-realization?" It's a stick figure—quickly eliminated by one swipe of Miss Harris' eraser.

"Self-what?" sneers Vida, my old A & W boss. "If she's got time to loll around writin' some piece of crap book about how hard it is to be a mother," she pauses to let the laughter in the moist crowded room die down, "then she's got time to find a job!"

Ranting about my "negative animus" and waving his copy

of *Swim with the Sharks,* my old therapist leaps up to give me a big thumbs down. A hail of splattering produce rains down from a balcony bursting with bawdy peasantry. And, furtively fanning away the tell-tale haze of Columbian Sublime, the entire Student Loan Commission nods in sanctimonious contempt.

As the mayhem heaves itself into giggling sobs, a thin cracking voice pierces the self-satisfied silence. Out of the crowd—like a Quaker at Meeting—rises my mother. "I am so disappointed in all of you," she rasps through angry tears. "Why can't you be more like Joan—she's just trying to live up to her full potential!"

The tribunal falls into a chagrined silence.

"But—but—" sputters my born-again ex, "without our vigilantes—I mean, our vigilance—she's a danger to herself and others. Without repression there is no law and order!"

Launching from its nest in Chinette's tower of hair, a re-animated rodent pelt sails across the room to bring down the bible-thumper. "Look at my babies!" Chinette leaps up on the evidence table and points to a dozen kids who are following Torgo's lead and dog-piling my ex. "They wouldn't even be here if I hadn't fully explored *my* human potential! If what you stand for is order," suddenly her bowie knife nails Dr. Laura's pink collar to the wall, "then I say, let there be anarchy!"

The balcony explodes into "ANARCHY NOW!" "BURN BABY BURN!" and "BOY WAS I *TOISTY!*" Half-incarnated man is rousing some half-incarnated rabble with a speech about "Asylum for the Parentally Incorrect!" Linda and Mary are running an overhead projector presentation on my new job description and Stewart's at the piano bar surrounded by men in hot pants singing *"People will Say We're In Love,"* while Spartacus and Poncho Villa bust down a wall with the Übermütter so Moses can let his people go. Pinochet heads for the rear exit, but Kathleen Cleaver bars the door.

Justice—or at least a clump of hotheads strapped for a tyranny to overturn—was on my side. But I knew it was up to me now to make being a mother fit with being myself.

I could almost hear the snap and tear of ethereal membranes, as I wrenched my psyche away from constant attention to Graham's needs. Disentangled at last, the prophecy of doom gripped me. What if once I dropped the ball and chain of parenting I didn't want to pick it up again?

I pictured poor Graham huddled in some squalid corner, ragged and wild-eyed, with nothing but the burnt-out shell of a Gameboy to defend his share of the cat food. "Graham! Guess what? The Gypsies are here! Sounds like quite a life they've got planned for you! And Mommy sure could use the two dollars!"

To defy this prediction of inevitable negligence, I summoned my superpowers of rationalization. Why, just the year before, I'd had surgery followed by six weeks of recovery. Graham didn't get much homeschooling then!

What if I were called to jury duty? Or I had three or four more children? What if a mudslide crushed the house? Any one of these would take far more time away from Graham than my writing would. My! There were endless justifications for redirecting some of the 168 hours per week that were entirely dedicated to Graham.

Like an alcoholic with nine years sobriety, I feared that first draft. But I knew from experience that if the rules won't bend, the bent will rule.

I went to work on the outline, sweating paranoid bullets that I might be caught enjoying it too much. And beating myself up because I wasn't teaching Graham a Basque festival song or enchanting him with a Kabuki version of the Iliad in Origami.

The first time I discovered I'd worked right through the Bookmobile's weekly visit I was aghast. Oh my god, the prophesy! I was indeed failing him! But after awhile, I was able to take the lack of clean socks and the serial dinner burning in stride. Eventually a new way of life arose from the ashes of the old. Maybe not better. But not worse, and definitely more comfortable. Like that old locomotive-car of my dream. It may have looked strange from the outside, but it had its own internal logic.

The years of enchantment were over. Like Rip Van Winkle, personhood was waking up from a nine year coma. The omni-mother was gone, but so was her chronic depression. In spite of the cold, burned or forgotten dinners, Graham seemed content with his new less attentive but happier mom.

After a few weeks I felt good in a way I had not felt in ages. As if I'd been a fish out of water and someone had thrown me back in. Now I could remember what my tail and fins were for. I was calmer around Graham, able to enjoy our time together more fully. I was more whole now.

I knew that creativity, like crime, doesn't pay. I knew the sensible thing would have been to jump right into that commuter pod car and let it take me to a job, dropping off Graham at childcare along the way.

And perhaps that time would still come, but for now I wanted to work on that old funky film projector/espresso machine engine. For now it fit our lives better.

Maybe I could fix it up a bit. Make it run a little more smoothly. And give it a nice comfortable cab, so I could sit up front—right between my unfinished dream friend in the driver's seat and Chinette, riding shotgun.

EPILOGUE:
JOI DU MERE ORDINAIRE

(or Hey, Get Me a Flashlight—
There's Some Neat Stuff on the Dark Side!)

*in which Joan travels beyond the
Valley of the Perfect Mother...*

"All I want is a path!" I muttered, wading through a sea of Lego's and Kapla blocks like a lumbering Godzilla. My mind was on Linda's imminent arrival. We were going to finish the book this weekend, and my house was still a mess.

I was just about to kick a plastic Viking man across the room, when Graham stepped in. "Who can hear my thoughts?" he asked with a worried look.

"You mean—read your mind? No one can read your mind."

"What about God?"

Oh. This was quite a departure from the practical concerns of the previous years, like, "When you're dead, how do I bury you?" and "Will I be bald?" Questions regarding the female deity he believed in always made me feel inadequate. They deserved rich thoughtful Rabbi-like answers I didn't have.

"Yes," I began tentatively. "God can hear our thoughts. But not the way people hear us when we talk. God doesn't just hear what you're thinking—she hears all the thoughts that came before. Every thought you've ever had, and all your feelings too." This seemed to be getting easier, as if someone were telling me what to say.

"If every thought is a candle, then each of us is a mountain covered with candles. And each one got its flame from the one before. So when you have a bad thought, God knows what made you sad enough to think it. God understands."

He'd probably just been wondering what makes a walkie-talkie work, but I was grateful for an excuse to reassure him that a universal force was in his corner. We all needed some assurance that somebody—somewhere—understood us, even if we couldn't understand ourselves.

I pushed open the attic windows to air out the room, and checked for any sign of Linda's little white Honda. Below, a dozen cats played hide and seek in the sweet pea and blackberry vines that climbed the willows and buried the forgotten toys that lay about like fallen soldiers. *How did I get here?* I asked myself, suddenly feeling a pang of sadness for my old life with Linda.

This new life of full-time motherhood was so different! But no, I wouldn't go back. *I was different now, too.*

Parenthood works in strange ways. First it rips you into little pieces and then it puts you back together like a Picasso, with your nose on the back of your head. It may look strange but sometimes it actually feels like everything's in the right place.

As I turned back to my bed-making, I was already feeling giddy just imagining Linda's opening vaudeville line as she stumbled through the door—*Do you realize there's no Hilton in Dutch Flat?* —or something.

Seeing Linda was for me what a Broadway musical is for other people. I was hungry for the panorama of pathos, the bold choreography, the maudlin solos. It was the fifth of July, but with Linda coming it felt like Christmas.

I was excited about working on the book with her in person rather than through the mail. But I think I would have enjoyed doing anything with Linda. Digging ditches, pressing uniforms. As long as I could talk to her.

But it was only in the last year that Linda and I had tunneled under that great wall that separated us, that wall that defined what was and was not safe to talk about—even between best friends.

Now we were once again enjoying the trust we'd denied ourselves for so long—that special unconditional acceptance that made it harder for me to condemn myself. I loved the warm rush I felt knowing what her response would be even before I actually confided in her. My viewpoint would shift from judgmental to empathic simply by listening to my thoughts the way she would. That convoluted, but dependable route to self-acceptance meant I had one less enemy—*me*.

At last I heard her pulling up the gravel driveway, and I ran down to give her a hug. She brought news of New York and Los Angeles, and promised a real prime rib dinner. I had stocked up on every aberration of snack food available, so cooking would not interrupt our three-day writing frenzy.

The only time we had to act like mothers was when Graham broke the bathroom light with an errant water balloon, and Jack had his first bike crash—minor, but still traumatic. Most of the time they were happily occupied and we ignored them completely, thanking the gods that they got along so well.

In the evenings we talked a little about the old days. Before our mutual motherhood. When Linda mentioned the stuffed bunny I used to have, I almost spit my Pink Vodka Surprise across the room.

Soft and floppy, it was usually wedged face down between two couch cushions. For years we pretended this ragged animal was the child Linda had abandoned and I had reluctantly taken in out of a sense of duty.

I would chide her about her neglect, and she would defend her right to pursue her self-actualization unfettered—to follow her creative impulses and fleeting passions wherever they led. Then we would laugh until we couldn't breathe. Little did we know that in a few years we would come face to face with the awesome power these seemingly ludicrous stereotypes wielded in the collective psyche of motherhood.

Perhaps more startling was the fact that we found ourselves embracing opposite extremes of the parenthood/personhood dichotomy. Embracing them so fiercely in fact, that each of us at times looked like a caricature of the other one's rejected half.

Over the months of writing the book, Linda and I had been able to get a closer look at our personal and cultural demons. Examining our adversaries had changed them. What had once been a menacing horde of internal dictators was now just a road crew of disgruntled flagmen, wagging their conflicting signs along the Superego-highway.

After a grueling twelve-hour day of rewriting, Linda was getting changed for our big dinner out. I tossed some pillows onto the futons I had wedged together to form a bed for her, "Here's some off Graham's bed."

"Thanks, but what's he going to use?"

"Oh, he doesn't sleep in that bed."

"He doesn't sleep in his bed? What—do you make him sleep outside on the porch?" she laughed.

"No, he sleeps in there."

"In your bed? I thought he was fine now."

"He is fine. He was never not fine!" I held my breath as she turned to re-organize her suitcase. Oh god, here it comes. She's going to pass judgment—in her own silent way. It's like I'm back on stage doing one of those trite outing scenes from the Socially Relevant Theatre of the 80's. Well, let's see—now should come the part where she shifts the conversation awkwardly to—how nice the quilt looks and how it feels like a bed and breakfast.

"Wow, this is just like a bed and breakfast!"

"Yeah, he still sleeps with me," I hissed, a fifth grader's *and whatcha gonna do about it* stuck in my throat.

"Okay. All right. I didn't mean to hurt your feelings," she whimpered, shrinking back as if I were brandishing a bullwhip.

"Oh, stop it! I can't stand it when you try to make me feel guilty for making you feel guilty. Just because I reacted in a perfectly normal human way to your stupid accusation!"

"It wasn't an accusation! I just—"

"God, just say it! You think I'm wrong! You think over half the world's population is wrong." I was trying too hard to hold my ground—what did belonging to a majority have to do with anything? Hadn't we both been trying to look at motherhood as an individual path?

"You're getting kind of defensive."

"Yeah, because you're being offensive. You could just ask— you know—ask a question like, well—*How does that work for you?*—or whatever. You might learn something!"

"I was trying. But you keep interrupting. I was going to ask you! If you'd let me." Her arms, hoisted like spears, now fell to her sides with great exasperated slaps. She blew out a tired horse sound to show how trying it was to have such an idiot for a friend. "Okay. So..." She collected herself. She was not going to stoop to my level. "When's he going to sleep in his own bed?"

"When he moves out, I guess. Shit! What kinda stupid question is that? God! This is what you've always done to me! You think I'm wrong, but you won't say it because you're too "nice." But you still do it! You judge me!"

"*I'm* judging??? Who sent me all those crappy Waldorf books in the mail, like if you just enlightened me enough I'd stop stealing my son's childhood or whatever that stupid Steinbaum says."

Suddenly we saw two little faces staring in at us from the hallway.

"Get out." I snarled. They slunk off, beaming. "God, I can't stand it." I started crying, lost my balance and sat down hard on the futons. "I just wish there was somebody in the world who wouldn't pass judgment."

"Well, maybe there isn't."

"Oh, thank you!"

"I mean—maybe we can't help it." Linda sat down beside me. "We just pass judgment 'cause we're stupid."

"But you *think* you *know*. That's why you judge."

"Yeah, Well, I'm stupid. Can you accept that about me?" She grabbed my hand the way she had during my Financial District breakdown so long ago. "I'm always going to judge, and so are you. But we don't have to act on it, right? I think I'm a bad mother a lot of the time—but do you see me trying to change into a better one because of that stupid judgment? No! Look right there! See how I just threw all Jack's stuff on the floor?" she stamps on the little heap of clothes for effect, "and spread mine out all nicely across the desk!"

"Yes," I felt myself smiling. "And I bet you don't even know where he is right now!"

"Know? I don't even care!" We laughed hard, and I suddenly realized we'd been fighting—for the first time in ten years. Actually fighting. At last—after a long, lonely decade, we were friends again.

I looked at Linda grinning and suddenly realized who she was. Underneath all that vulnerability and goofiness was a pittbull who had not let go of me during all these difficult years. Why would she do that? She didn't seem to understand me half the time. She didn't agree with my parenting. I certainly hadn't given her much of myself. But in spite of all that she loved me. And somehow she'd kept some kind of faith that I still loved her. I realized then that I knew as little about the mystery of friendship as I did about the enigma of motherhood.

When we got home from the Monte Vista Inn that night, Linda and I were really too tired to do anything with the kids, but we'd promised them sparklers.

I felt resentful about having to stay up one minute longer, and I let everyone know it by sighing dramatically as each of my attempts to light the damn things failed. Still, I enjoyed watching the boys race down the rickety porch, stabbing at the night. They were great friends. Playing as wildly and spontaneously as Linda and I did whenever we got together.

There was no one I was more myself around than Linda. It wasn't the best she brought out in me. Not my wisest or most mature self. It was something more fundamental. She brought out the child in me— the raw, uninhibited child. She brought out my passion for living.

I rubbed my aching neck as I shifted back into my protector role, trying to follow the dim galloping shapes. I always worried that one day someone would fall through one of those termite-infested planks.

All I could locate now were the sparklers and the high-pitched tinkling hysteria that seemed to emanate from them. But I stifled my usual litany of *"Lookouts"* and *"Don't jump too hards"* as I noticed Linda's face lighting up, taking it all in.

I suddenly realized that for all our guiding and teaching, it's our children who actually lead the way. Whether they're the ones we raise or the ones who live inside us—or even this one masquerading as a grownup who happened to be my best friend.

Poking around our shadows, they come banging into everything we've hidden. Their brilliant immediacy exposing secret fears and dusty dreams, giving us a chance to have a look around and see just who it is we're growing up to be.

To order a copy
of Motherhood Confidential
Email: JoanBechtel1@comcast.net
www.MotherhoodConfidential.com